THE CALMER **WAY TO FUTURE-PRO**
YOUR CAREER AND WELLBEING

STOP

SARAH
SPARKS

www.get-known.co.uk

To Theo, who never ceases to surprise and inspire me.
I am proud of the young man you have become

CONTENTS

PART 1

**The Problem:
What Happened to Me Can
Happen to You**

PART 2

THE SCALE OF THE STRESS PROBLEM

More than one in three adults (35%) say they are experiencing a lot of stress.[1]

Forty-two percent of workers face high stress in their jobs, negatively affecting their productivity, health and family stability:[2]

- 28% have difficulty concentrating

- 20% take longer to complete their work

- 15% have trouble reasoning or deciding

The top physical wellbeing risks impacting company performance are:[3]

- Stress: 67%

- Burnout: 46%

Forty-two percent of employees had experienced a decline in their mental health since the pandemic started.[4]

Seventy-six percent of US workers are experiencing burn-out symptoms.[5]

According to research, an estimated 91 million workdays are lost annually in the UK due to mental health disorders.[6]

The World Economic Forum estimates that by 2030, the cost of mental disorders to the global economy will reach $16 trillion – more than diabetes, respiratory disorders and cancer combined.[7]

By the time they reach the age of 30, 95% of workers in the UK will have been touched by mental health challenges– either their own or those of a friend, family member or co-worker. Three out of four will have personally experienced such a challenge. These individuals are also almost twice as likely as their older peers to be experiencing issues with their mental health *right now.*[8]

THIS BOOK IS FOR...

This book is for you if you:

- Are a strong achiever and work in a high-pressure, competitive environment

- Have a lot of responsibilities to juggle, both inside and outside of work

- Work long hours and still don't feel there are ever enough hours in the day

- Are driven and ambitious and want to progress in your career

- Find it difficult to relax or quieten your mind (even when you're on holiday)

- Have good intentions but struggle to find a work–life balance and to be fully present with your family/partner when you are at home

- Are getting tired of the constant demands

- Are beginning to feel spent.

Does any of this sound familiar? If so, you are in the right place.

What you really want is to find a better way of living and working, one in which you enjoy:

- More energy, focus and productivity

- A life that is more enjoyable and fun

- More calm

- More time to spend on yourself and your family

- Better physical and mental health and wellbeing.

I'm here to show you how to achieve that state in order to thrive in the long term across all areas of your life. I was once exactly where you are now, so I know how exhausting it can be. I wrote this book for my younger self. It's the book I wish I had read back when I was in my mid-thirties, working for Goldman Sachs. It's the book that might have prevented my burnout and the significant consequences that unfolded. It's the wake-up call I wish I'd had.

THIS BOOK WILL...

This is a simple book full of ideas that are quick and easy to do but which will take you from a life of constant stress and demands to one that is calmer and more enjoyable.

It will help you to recognise the warning signs of burnout, explain what can happen if you ignore those signs and, more importantly, give you easy and achievable tips on what you can do to prevent it.

I'll share with you four key areas you need to master and lots of practical steps you can apply immediately, no matter how busy you are, to improve your current situation and help you to have better relationships, health and wellbeing. It will show you a path towards more happiness and joy.

Plus, you'll perform better at work and be more successful due to your:

- Better self-esteem

- Better concentration, focus and productivity

- Better communication and relationships

- Better creative thinking, problem-solving and decision-making.

The book is full of real people's stories – people who have found a sustainable way of working in very demanding corporate environments and are thriving. You can, too, if you take action now.

Some of my advice you already know on some level, but right now you're not doing anything about it. That's about to change.

If you read this whole book and agree with everything in it but don't change your behaviour, it will have been a complete waste of your time. In fact, if that is typical of your behaviour– you read a good book and think the ideas are great but don't do anything as a consequence– can I suggest you stop reading now? This book is not for you.

This book is for action takers. People who are sick and tired of feeling sick and tired and want to do something about it.

I'm fully aware that the last thing you need right now is another commitment to add to all the other demands in your life. I get it. The micro-steps in this book will have a profound impact on your peace of mind and effectiveness in all aspects of your life over time.

Before we begin, get yourself a new journal. Alternatively, there is a free workbook on my website where all the micro-steps and more in-depth exercises are included. Get it from **www.sarahsparks.co.uk/ideas/download-your-workbook-here**

Are you ready? If so, let's get started.

MEET SARAH SPARKS

Since suffering burnout in her late thirties, losing her prestigious job and marriage, she's focused her career on helping others create the building blocks to prosper, grow and flourish at work and in life.

Sarah Sparks is:

- An award-winning executive coach, author and speaker who specialises in helping senior leaders in the corporate world reduce stress and avoid burnout

- Known for getting results fast; after a recent talk she gave at a large city institution (talking about 'Thriving at Work', with an audience of over 1,000), 94% said they would immediately implement what they learnt

- One of RBS, Citigroup and Bank of America Merrill Lynch's top coaches

- A 'thought provocateur', ensuring her clients manage their stress and stay away from distress

- Founder of 'Choose to Thrive', which she started

after a finance career that included working at a senior level at Goldman Sachs

- A respected voice and contributor to publications such as the *FT* and *You!* magazine, and Radio 4

- A qualified yacht master who enjoys messing about on boats as often as she is able

- A mum to a gorgeous son who never ceases to challenge and inspire her. After years of infertility and many rounds of failed IVF, and being put on HRT, she conceived naturally at the age of 46.

And another thing: she starts her day with a cold shower and believes it has helped build up her resilience.

PART 1

THE PROBLEM: WHAT HAPPENED TO ME CAN HAPPEN TO YOU

"If you always do what you've always done, you'll always get what you've always got."

HENRY FORD

Even before the COVID-19 outbreak, the World Health Organization said, 'Stress is a global health epidemic'.[9] Stress is the epidemic of the 21st century, brought on by the way we live our lives, where there are huge amounts of uncertainty, continuous change and the 'always on' mentality.

The hectic speed of life has exacerbated the situation. Our brains are not designed for such a demanding experience. We were designed for a slower pace and greater simplicity in a life where survival was key, so feeding and procreating were high on the agenda.

That is a place very far from most people's lives these days– which are driven by a hunger for more. More money, more responsibilities, more status, more adventures, more experiences. Bigger and better than anything that has come before us.

It is a life where success is measured in what you have – the large house, the smart car, the exotic holidays, the kids in private school, the private trainer, exclusive restaurants – and not by who you are.

If COVID-19 has done anything, perhaps it has allowed people to stop and think about what's really important to them and given them an option to create a different life. Instead of a full life – a fulfilling life.

A few facts about mental health (in case you need persuading)

One in four of us will experience a mental health challenge in our lifetime. Worse than that: a 2019 UK study about mental health at work, conducted on behalf of the organisation Business in the Community, stated that for those under 30, the figure is three out of four![10]

The reality is: it's all of us.

We all have mental health, just like we all have physical health, and both go up and down with life's events, but though they are equally important, we don't treat them both the same.

Health and Safety legislation is very clear that our work environments should be safe physically. But they should be safe for our mental health too.

Back in 2017, Theresa May, the then UK prime minister, commissioned Lord Denis Stevenson and Paul Farmer (CEO of Mind) to look at the state of mental health at work. In their report, called *Thriving at Work*, they concluded that 'the UK faces a significant mental health challenge'.[11]

- 15% of people at work have symptoms of an existing mental health condition.

- 300,000 people with a long-term mental health problem lost their jobs each year, and at a much higher rate than those with physical health conditions.

- The human cost is huge, with poor mental health having an impact on the lives of many individuals and those around them.

- There is a large annual cost to employers: between £33bn and £42bn, with over half of the cost coming from presenteeism (when individuals are less productive due to poor mental health in work) and additional costs from sickness absence and staff turnover.

- The cost of poor mental health to the government was between £24bn and £27bn, including benefits, fall in tax revenues and costs to the NHS.

- The cost to the economy of poor mental health was between £74bn and £99bn per year.

Back in 2018, a report by *The Lancet* estimated the cost of mental health at $16tn[12]; it will no doubt be much more now. That's huge!

In a *Sunday Times* article in 2016, it was estimated that three out of four bankers were suffering from insomnia, panic attacks, headaches and depression caused by work-related stress.[13] Three out of four! That is staggering and very concerning.

According to the Health and Safety Executive, mental health conditions are now the number one cause of sickness,[14] and in its Labour Force Survey (2009/10–2011/12) the predominant causes of work-related stress, depression, or anxiety were:

1. Workload, and in particular tight deadlines

2. Too much responsibility

3. Too much work[15]

Are any of the above familiar to you or someone you know?

Shockingly, suicide is the leading cause of death for men between the ages of 15 and 49, and men account for four out of five cases – a terrible statistic.

I have personally known of four people who have lost their lives due to mental ill health in the last couple of years and this has been one of the catalysts for me to get out there and bang the drum about the issue.

The reality is that work seems to be taking over our lives.

Over-extending ourselves seems to be a way of life, but we are not biologically designed to be in this high-stress mode all the time. Somehow, we have got it into our heads that to be productive and successful we need to work hard and be on the go all the time, when in fact quite the opposite is true. We are human beings not human doings, after all.

How are you coping with today's fast pace and pressure?

Are you:

- Working longer hours?

- Taking on more and more?

- Sacrificing sleep to get things done?

- Sacrificing your key relationships to pay the mortgage?

- Putting your own health at the bottom of the pile?

Be honest with yourself. What will happen if nothing changes? What will be the consequences then?

Many people are living to work rather than working to live. Aren't we meant to work so that we can enjoy life? Many of us seem to have got things mixed up and are sacrificing enjoyment and our health for work.

Chronic stress is insidious and creeps up on you.

The scale of the problem today

What's happening right now?

Maybe you are like many of my clients when I first meet them. They are running around trying to do everything. They may seem on the surface to be doing really well at work, having an impressive title, being promoted often, earning lots of money, being more successful than they dreamed possible.

And yet underneath they are running to keep up. As they try to hold it all together and appear swan-like on the surface, their legs are spinning under the water just to stay afloat. Often, they're worried about dropping a ball and being found out. Some of these people have even told me that they keep expecting someone to tap them on the shoulder and say 'you're a fraud' – imposter syndrome is ever present.

You're working long hours and you know it's not good for you, but you convince yourself it's not for long and if you can just push through this last bit, you'll be able to take your foot off the accelerator and relax.

But that finish line never comes, and you find yourself exhausted and continuing to 'push through'. There is always something that needs your attention that you *have* to do. No let-up. Just day after day of the same old grind.

On good days, you convince yourself that you'll get to the gym, and it's all manageable – everyone else is doing it, so it must be OK. Besides, it's just what's expected of you in your job, working in this type of organisation. If you're going to do well, then it must be done; if you don't keep up and pull your weight, you'll be the first for the chop when redundancies come, and you can't afford for that to happen.

You have commitments, a mortgage, bills to pay, credit card debt to pay off, holidays you've promised your other half, that car you've set your heart on, that wedding or special occasion you've been saving up for. You can't afford to lose your job because all this would disappear, and you couldn't face that.

And so you're up early every day and from the moment you wake, you're on it. Busy. Processing emails, juggling tasks at home and at work, multitasking every moment and trying to claim back every minute that feels like it's slipping through your fingers.

You hate it. You know you can't be doing your best work.

On bad days it feels hopeless. You're just not up to it; not clever enough, not smart enough. You don't believe it's possible to do everything– but there must be some-thing wrong with you, as others seem to be able to. You're stupid. Pathetic. A waste of space.

Then you give yourself a talking-to… and you're on it again, taking more on. You're good at problem-solving and, besides, you want to prove yourself. What do they say? 'If you want to get a job done, give it to a busy person.'

But inside you are thinking, 'Why did I do that? I'm drown-ing here.' You just have to get on and get through this. Head down.

Maybe it hasn't even occurred to you that you can say no or ask for help. You've been a self-sufficient insecure over-achiever since your time began on this earth.

It doesn't have to be this way

If any of this sounds familiar – then please know you're not alone. There are plenty of people out there doing the same. It's normal today, right? I did it too – and I'll tell you more about that in the next chapter.

"When you work in a large high-profile organisation with lots of bright, intelligent people, you want to succeed, and you end up putting a lot of pressure on yourself. I wanted to be successful. I wanted to earn enough money to support my family. I didn't want to go through the things that my dad went through in terms of redundancy and not being able to provide. And so I have worked very hard to avoid that. I always thought the harder you work, the more successful you'd be.

"Working in a competitive culture (which is no bad thing) means if you're not doing it, then somebody else will be. You put pressure on yourself to be 20 times better than everybody else. And therefore, if you find it difficult to switch off (like I do), the chances of you burning out are quite high; because you like what you're doing, and you can see the not insignificant rewards are within reach.

"That was true, in my case, because I really loved the role. It was challenging, but I was working 15-hour days. Typically, over the two-and-a-half-year period that I did the role, rather stupidly as I think now, my

alarm went off at 4:30 in the morning. I would get up, have breakfast, go to the station, get the 5:55 train. I'd be at my desk in Canary Wharf before 7:00. I would sensibly leave the office at sort of 5:00, or something like that. But I would come home, have tea, and then I'd work again, and I'd have several calls with leadership in the evening.

"But the thing is, of course, I was enjoying it, and I was being successful and productive. And I got promoted to director. Outwardly, everything was good. Earning more money and providing for my family felt good. But there was nothing left in the tank and I was empty. Admittedly, nobody was telling me to work the 15-hour days, but then again, nobody was telling me not to.

"The knock-on impact was a massive lack of sleep, very low mood, and getting no enjoyment out of life. You sink back into yourself, and you're not a good husband, and you're not a good dad because you're there, but you're not really present."

Nick Baber, Director and Chief Operating Officer, Professional Services

But what I want to point out to you is that it doesn't have to be that way.

Have you noticed there are people out there who seem to be able to take things in their stride? When things go wrong, they may have a short-term setback but they soon find a way of getting back on track.

Just imagine what that's like.

Imagine waking up in the morning after a good night's sleep, feeling energised and clear about how you want your day to go and already feeling on top of your plans before it even starts. There is a grounded knowingness about you. A gravitas and a confidence.

Imagine smiling more and enjoying life. Your work brings you a sense of satisfaction, and you still have time for the things and people that matter. You have time for exercise. You have time for your nearest and dearest. You have time for interests outside of work that bring you joy.

All in all, you are happier and in better physical and mental health. Life is on a roll; you're successful and feeling good. Now you're not just a high achiever – you are a high performer.

A high achiever is great at focusing on getting things done and ticking things off the to-do list. Sound familiar? The high performer, however, is different. They get huge satisfaction from getting the *right* things done: those things that represent the best use of their time and where they can make the biggest impact. It's a completely different way of looking at things.

A high performer is what I call a 'Thriver' not a 'Striver'.

Thrivers have the resilience to get through each day, whatever is thrown at them. Strivers, on the other hand, are running on empty before the day has even started and don't have any spare capacity in the system to deal with what's coming.

And the thing is: the Strivers and Thrivers not only *do* things differently, they also *think* differently, and as a consequence they get different results.

Which one do you want to be?

CHAPTER 1

MY STORY

"If only I had known then what I know now."

SARAH SPARKS

Before I go on, let me take you back to July 1995.

I'm sitting in a familiar hospital office. This one was dark with oak panelled walls and there's a stern yet familiar face opposite me. It belongs to an Asian man with a sharp pointy nose and thick black hair.

'You know why you're back at the Priory, Sarah, don't you? You've been completely overdoing it again. Long, long hours, skipping breakfast, living off coffee, lunch on the run, using wine to relax, no breaks, working weekends!

It's not surprising that you're back here. Did you not learn anything from your last admission? This time, I'm going to have to keep you in for longer and put you back on medication. Sarah, this can't keep happening. This has to stop!'

'I know, I know! I just don't have a choice,' I say fervently.

'Of course you have a choice. Everyone has a choice! Does it say in your contract that you have to work these crazy hours? No, it doesn't! Does it say in your contract that you're not entitled to breaks and you have to work weekends? No, it doesn't! Does it say in your contract that you should work so hard you make yourself ill? *No, it doesn't!* You have a choice, Sarah. You're just not choosing wisely right now!'

Have you ever had a wake-up call?

Sitting in the room of my consultant psychiatrist, having that conversation – that was my wake-up call.

It had genuinely never dawned on me before that I had a choice in how I lived my life. I know that sounds rather ridiculous now, but somehow I had grown up to believe I had to conform and that if I was asked to do something in my job, I had to do it. Never once had it occurred to me that I could say no or ask for help.

If I couldn't do something, I thought it meant I wasn't clever or smart or quick enough, or working hard enough.

Not once did I think that maybe the request wasn't reasonable. And so I never said no, and I never challenged authority figures. I just worked harder and harder so I could succeed.

Hearing myself now, I want to laugh. It sounds so ridiculous.

That conversation with my consultant (in my late thirties) *was* life changing, but it wasn't an instantaneous fix. It took years and years to get well again, and even more years to put into practice this new-found realisation that I had a choice. It sounds so simple, doesn't it? And yet it wasn't easy. But I know now there is a lot you can do immediately that makes a difference; more about that in later chapters.

So how on earth did I find myself in such a place?

I had been working at Goldman Sachs for several years and I thought I was on a roll. I worked hard, enjoyed it, got paid well and got promoted. So I took on more, worked harder, got paid even more and got promoted again, and so it kept happening.

I was on a high (though there was always this little voice inside me worrying about being 'found out'). To this day, I can remember the pride on my father's face when I told him I had just been promoted to Executive Director at the bank. I had a beautiful Lotus Elan soft-top car, holidayed wherever the fancy took me – mostly hot places – and thought I was the bee's knees.

Life really was falling into place. I had recently got married to the man of my dreams. We met in July and got married in December. It felt so right, yet the reality was that we didn't really know each other very well, and as I was working such long hours, we didn't get to hang out much.

I tried to be the perfect everything– wife, hostess, lover, housewife– while at the same time being the perfect employee, boss, colleague and friend.

I insisted on doing my fair share of cooking, entertaining and housework, which meant that my weekends were full-on too, while still trying to catch up on work when I had a moment to spare. This was clearly not a sustainable recipe for romance or success, but I kept on going. All I kept thinking was 'I need to keep pushing on and pushing on through.' But the reality was that something had to give.

And here's the thing. Something *was* giving, but it was so insidious and the changes so imperceptible that I had no idea my ability to function was being compromised.

I didn't notice until much later that I couldn't focus and concentrate like I used to, nor could I think straight. My sleep was deteriorating, and I was getting short and snappy with my loved ones. Not helpful at any time, but especially not in what was meant to be the honeymoon period of a new marriage.

Getting married in my thirties meant that I didn't want to leave procreating for too long either, so as newly-weds we enjoyed every opportunity to 'get close and personal'.

Life was fun, and I loved it. I loved being adored at home and respected and admired at work. I felt incredible and believed I was invincible. I can see now that my need for external admiration and validation was part of the problem, but back then it just felt great.

I really took to married life and the additional commitments that came with it. The mortgage, the shared bank accounts, the strong desire for my husband to be successful too – which meant I was quite willing to lend his business money. These didn't feel burdensome at the time, but I can see now that I was just piling on responsibilities and commitments.

I was working really hard at the time, having just been promoted to the role of co-head of Financial Regulation for everything outside the US. It was a huge responsibility, and I must confess I felt completely out of my depth. From the day I was promoted, I was expected to know the answers in this highly technical area. There was no way that was possible, but at the same time, it didn't occur to me to push back.

I started to work even longer hours, being at my desk before 7am and often catching a taxi home at 11pm. I didn't have time to eat during the day and lived off cups and cups of coffee, and maybe a sandwich on the fly. When I got home, all I was fit for was a glass of wine ('make it a big one') and a snack. Cheese and biscuits were a favourite supper.

On the one hand, I felt exhilarated by the cut and thrust of what I was doing and the giddy heights I had climbed… and on the other I felt exhausted and wretched and didn't know what to do with myself. Adding to that, sleep was a bit of a problem. I fell asleep pretty easily, probably because of all the wine, but would wake up after a few hours with my mind racing.

I had a very unhealthy attitude towards sleep. I thought it was a complete waste of time. 'I can sleep when I'm dead' was my motto. Sleep is one of those things I protect like a hawk these days, but back then I let anything – and anyone – steal it from me.

Have you ever felt that your life is not in your control? That someone else was spinning the hamster wheel and there was no way you could get off? It became apparent over time that it wasn't just sleep I was allowing others to steal from me.

I remember one day distinctly.

I am sitting in the back of a taxi, racing along the King's Road. It's so early in the morning that there's hardly another car in sight on this normally jam-packed road. It's going to be a stunning summer day – the birds already know it and are making a jubilant racket, which I hear through the open window.

This peaceful, glorious day in the making is in sharp contrast to the feeling inside me. I feel sick. The thought of breakfast makes me want to retch. My eyes are sore from tiredness and I stare at the pile of papers on my lap, trying to make sense of them. But nothing is going in. I'm starting to panic.

I have to get through these papers I'm staring at, but the words dance around the page and don't make any sense. I keep looking up, then trying to start again, but it's not working. Now I'm really panicking.

I haven't had much sleep, because the phone rang a couple of times in the night– traders from Tokyo, calling to ask my permission to do trades they had already done, and now I'm left trying to sort out the mess.

I must get hold of my boss; we'll call him Slippery Jim. He is slippery all right, one of those plump New Yorkers with a sweaty handshake and a blotchy complexion. He reminds me of Danny DeVito, but without the personality. And I need his help.

As I arrive at the office, there he is, coming out of the elevator.

'Hey Jim, do you have a minute?'

'What's up, Sarah? Why are you interrupting my cawfee? Sorry, no time today: back-to-back meetings. I'm sure you can handle it. Give me a call at the end of the day and tell me it's done.'

What an arsehole! What a fucking arsehole! How dare he walk away and not even hear me out? I *never* ask for help, and he's walking away... What am I going to do?

The next thing I remember is being in the Priory. I don't know how I got there. (I later found out that I collapsed in the office and the company doctor was called.) I do vaguely remember the doctor saying to me, 'Don't worry; we are going to put you in cotton wool for a while.'

The first thing I felt in the hospital was huge relief: I didn't have to wade through any complicated regulatory papers or be at the beck and call of others. I did feel very unwell, completely spaced out and not able to function, but somehow I also felt safe.

I didn't have to do anything. My bed was made, my room was cleaned, my food was provided, and all I had to do was turn up to group or individual therapy sessions. Those took huge effort, and I turned up to most of them in a zombie-like state, but nonetheless, just having this small demand placed on me got me out of bed.

I was in the hospital for months this second time, and I didn't know what to do with myself. I was a blithering, crying ball of nothingness, or that's how it felt. I couldn't read a book or a newspaper – words swam on the page and nothing would go in – but after some experimenting, I did find two things I could do. One was jigsaw puzzles, and the other was needlepoint.

I calculated that I was able to do about 1 cm2 of needlepoint in the time it took to listen to an episode of *The Archers* – approximately 12 minutes. I spent hours and hours counting my days, doing needlepoint, and I still have it framed in my mother's house. Each time I look at it I see the hours in the abyss. My brain had shut down.

The months passed and, sometime after that conversation with my consultant, I was allowed home. I don't remember much about going home, but one conversation is emblazoned on my memory.

It's a week since I left the hospital, and my husband and I are having breakfast together, with the Sunday newspapers. Freshly baked croissants, homemade strawberry jam – courtesy of his mother – and freshly brewed coffee. The words in the newspaper are still swimming around, but I'm enjoying flicking through the pictures in the colour supplements.

Suddenly, my husband drops the bomb. 'You're not the woman I married.'

What? I'm confused and scared. *Of course I'm not the woman you married.*

I had been feeling pretty good about the fact that I had finally decided to start making choices about me and how I lived my life. Surely that was a good thing? But for him, it meant he was going to be getting a completely different Sarah: one who looked out for herself and put herself on the priority pile for the first time in her life.

I get it. I had effectively changed the contract – the unspoken psychological contract we had both signed up for – and I had done it without consultation. I knew this was going to be hard to reconcile, but I knew I had to do it for me.

I had no idea of the devastating consequences it would have for our relationship.

It was over a year before I went back to work. And it was a hard call. I had been so traumatised by the whole experience that even thinking about going back to work would bring on a panic attack.

I practised doing the commute, going to the office, and just sitting in reception to see if I could do it. It took me several attempts to make it into the building but eventually I did it… and so began my return to work.

I didn't return to the same job – which was just as well, as I wouldn't have been able to do it. I had a new job, a new boss and none of the old gremlins. It helped, but I did experience a huge level of shame. No one asked me how I was, because they didn't really know how to talk about mental illness back then. I am not sure it's improved much since.

I felt very alone and isolated. I don't remember my new boss talking to me about it much, either. I felt a huge pressure to perform, just as I had done before. But the reality was: I couldn't.

My brain and body would take many more years to recover before I could perform at a high level. A doctor had told me it would take five years to recover fully, and I just scoffed at the idea. But they were right!

Meanwhile, there were other things going on with my body too. I was 32 when we got married, and both my husband and I wanted to have a family. We tried with no success, so along the way we explored in-vitro fertilisation (IVF). It was one of the hardest things I have ever had to do, from both a physical and a psychological point of view.

If you've experienced it, you know – and if you haven't, I hope you never have to. I had no idea how my stressful life was impacting my ability to conceive and fulfil my dream of having a family. I ended up going through six failed IVF attempts, and it nearly killed me.

The emotional roller-coaster you go through with IVF is excruciating, and the disappointment and grief were overwhelming at times. Even to this day, I still have moments when I weep for the children I never had and the experiences that would have come with them. The ups and the downs. All of which I would welcome with open arms if only I could turn the clock back.

When I did return to work, I started to notice just how many of the people around me were on the same treadmill. Working hard, with responsible jobs and huge amounts of pressure, working crazy hours, doing anything and everything to have the trappings of success.

Trappings. What an appropriate word. The large homes with large mortgages, nice cars, smart new clothes, forking out for lavish holidays several times a year, kids (if they had them) going to expensive public schools, expensive hobbies. They had everything except the things that mattered: time for themselves and their loved ones.

There is a huge cost to having it all.

I saw many people in that environment with broken relationships, bitter divorces, and fighting over money and kids. The protracted court cases. The years of animosity, anger and jealousy. The impact that had on their stress levels while they still tried to hold down their responsible, pressurised jobs.

Their health often suffered, too.

Was it worth it? Only they would be able to answer that, but for me it was a high price to pay and one I wouldn't have chosen, if only I had known.

What my mental breakdown taught me was that it didn't have to be that way.

I'm sure you'd agree that the world has changed over the last few decades as technology and information have connected the world. And yet the way we work hasn't changed.

We're just trying to work harder and harder and longer and longer to keep up. That would be OK if we were machines, but we're not. We are human *beings* not human *doings*.

Fundamentally, the way we work doesn't work!

This is why I wanted to write this book: to share the small practical steps that make a difference. Steps that, if you take them every day, will improve your current situation and, over time, will help you to change the way you work and thrive – not just at work, but also in your health, wealth, and relationships.

You have to wake up to the signs and make some wise, conscious choices. But the thing is, once you start to notice and understand, you can no longer kid yourself and pretend you don't know. You are changed for ever.

My mantra these days is that 'I choose to thrive' and I will do what I need to do every day so that I can *be* my best. Don't get me wrong; I'm not perfect and don't always get it right, but no longer can I hide in denial about what I am doing to my body and brain and how that impacts my effectiveness.

What do you want in your life?

As with investing our money or spending it, if we look after and invest in ourselves rather than expending all our energy for short-term gains, we can, if we are lucky, live a long life reaping the rewards.

I set up my company, Choose to Thrive, to support dynamic, smart professionals who know there's more they can do to be their best and to bring out the best in others.

My job is to lovingly provoke and challenge the status quo and help them make better choices so that they can choose to thrive.

I'm loving life these days. I do only the things I love, making a positive difference to people's lives. I talk to people all around the world about how to choose to thrive so that they can be their best selves and live their best life. So they can have success but without the stress.

I collaborate with respected colleagues in my field and share the latest thinking. I'm a sought-after coach and, when time allows, I work one to one with senior leaders in financial services companies to help them have greater impact and inspire others.

Between us, we can change the way we work... but it has to start with you.

CHAPTER 2

THE PROBLEMS AND WHAT I WISH I HAD KNOWN

"One of the other physiological signs to me of burnout is that I can't maintain focus on a task. Being able to multitask to a high degree was needed for my role. But it makes it increasingly hard to spot that sign of burnout, because your job demands it."

MID-THIRTIES WOMAN WORKING FOR INTERNATIONAL BANK

Do you feel stressed all the time? Has there been a time recently when you haven't felt stressed? How would you know, anyway? The truth is that for many people, chronic stress is the norm. What would you say if I asked you, 'Is stress good or bad?'

The answer is: it's both.

Humans are designed for acute episodes of stress as part of our survival strategy. We have an awesome system that kicks in when we are in danger that gives us supernatural powers.

The stress hormones that are released when we are in danger kick off the fight, flight or freeze response and shut down the immune, digestive and reproductive systems. This works well if you have to run away from a sabre-toothed tiger, but not so well if you experience severe levels of stress daily.

The chances are, if you have a job with a lot of responsibility, your stress response is being triggered so many times a day that it starts to feel normal, which is why it's difficult to tell whether or not you are in that state. The consequences of chronic stress start off subtly, but they are likely to be causing you all sorts of mischief.

If you're experiencing any of the following symptoms, then the chances are you might be experiencing an episode of chronic stress.

Symptoms of chronic stress

- Brain fog
- Inability to think straight
- Low mood
- Shallow breathing
- Exhaustion
- Cynicism
- Inefficacy
- Forgetfulness
- Tearfulness
- Mood swings
- Numbness of feeling
- Low levels of concentration
- Lack of creativity
- Difficulties with problem-solving
- Feelings of anxiousness
- Insomnia or poor sleep
- Erratic eating
- Excessive worrying
- Self-criticism
- Impaired concentration
- Anger
- Irritability
- Detachment

We all experience stress in different ways. You may experience many of the signs listed, or you may only experience a few. Do any of them sound familiar? If so, you are not alone.

"When tough things happened, at work and home, I just thought I would try harder. I'd just keep pushing through. I'd work smarter. I'd think things through properly. It always worked before; it would be fine. Then slowly, during 2013, things imperceptibly started to decline, but I didn't know what was going on. It happened so slowly. I ignored the signs. But then they became more obvious; my chest started to tingle, my patience evaporated, my sleep was disturbed, my breath became a little shallower and quicker. I just kept on pushing myself harder. The doctor said, 'It happens to people like you.' There began what my kids called the Great Depression. It was mind-bendingly horrible, and it took some time to recover. But a full recovery and a better life, if approached with patience and an allowing attitude, is always there... if we can learn to ride the waves."

**DAVID TAPNACK, PARTNER AND
MENTAL HEALTH ADVOCATE, PwC**

Athletes know how to deal with stress.

If you were a professional athlete, you would be focusing on your recovery just as much as your training and performance. Athletes know that if they want to be at peak performance for a particular event, they need to plan and build up to the big day.

They do that by pushing themselves during training and then giving themselves and their muscles time to recover and grow. If they kept training without any recovery time, their performance would deteriorate.

The same is true in the business world, except that it's not recognised. If you want to be your best and have a sustainable high-performance strategy, you must build in rest and recovery. That brings down stress hormones and also builds your resilience.

The reality is that if you want to be your best, you have to rest.

Now, you might be happy with the status quo (although probably not, if you are still reading). You may already realise you will be heading for danger if nothing changes. My suspicion is that there are already things in your life that are suffering right now.

Maybe it's your health, relationships, career or finances. If that's the case, you have the power to change them – and, in fact, *only* you can do so. No one else can do this for you.

The whole thing is about implementation. Doing something different. After all:

"If you always do what you've always done, you'll always get what you've always got."

HENRY FORD

Now is the time to change. Don't wait for some health challenge to set you back. Don't wait for your relationship to fall apart to take some action. You don't need to wait.

So, if you have decided that you want to make changes in your life, let's get started with understanding what's going on under the bonnet, in our body and brain. If only I had known then what I know now, life would have been very different.

There was so much I didn't know back then. I don't think I was living under a rock, and I don't think you are either, but a lot of this knowledge is just not shared. Ever. Not within families, in schools, colleges or universities, or in the workplace.

And by the time you are considering your career– whether that is at 16, 18 or in your early twenties– it's too late. The habits are set in, the understanding (or lack of it) is established, and you go on your merry way doing the best you can.

On reflection, I think this is criminal. Why are we not teaching our kids and young adults the basics about stress, optimising their brains and maximising their potential?

Right now, with the recent COVID-19 crisis, all sorts of things are having to be rewritten. Let's hope this is one of them.

The good news is that it's not too late to learn about how your brain and body work. Even having a basic understanding can open your eyes to what's possible and make your life much easier and simpler.

Understanding some key facts about your physiology can really help you have 'more success without the stress', and who wouldn't want that? Imagine if, just by making some small shifts in your behaviour, you could open up your brain functions and be able to have peace of mind and maximise your potential. Wouldn't that be awesome?

I don't claim to be a scientist or an expert in brain function, but I have learnt the hard way about what doesn't work and the significant consequences that had on my young career and life. If only I had known those things, I could probably still be working at Goldman Sachs... if I chose to.

In this chapter, I'll share with you some of the basic things I didn't know that would have made all the difference.

Let me break this down into five key areas:

- How stress affects performance

- The stress response

- Stress hormones

- Communications model

- Brain facts

Stress and performance

I assumed in the past that stress was bad, and to be avoided if possible– but I couldn't avoid it, and the chances are that nor can you.

But I now know that stress is both good and bad. You need some stress/pressure to get out of bed in the morning, and some days will have more stress/pressure than others. You need a certain level of stress ('eustress') to perform at your best. It can be a real motivator and can galvanise you into action, sometimes allowing you to achieve things you never thought possible.

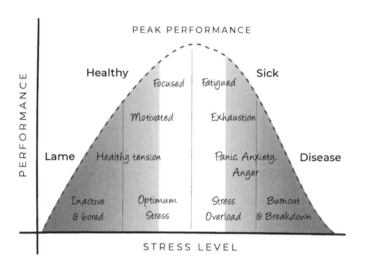

FIG 1. THE RELATIONSHIP BETWEEN STRESS AND PERFORMANCE.

What it shows is that if you put yourself under an optimal level of stress to induce peak performance, you would build resilience and be able to cope with additional pressure while still performing well.

However, too much stress can be detrimental – even fatal – if left unchecked.

Putting yourself under unhealthy levels of stress for prolonged periods leads to sickness and disease, resulting in exhaustion, panic, anxiety and burnout. It even causes people to take their own lives.

The stress response

What's going on in your body when the stress response is triggered?

Look at the graph below. It looks similar to the one above but is, in reality, a completely different matter. This time it is looking at stress hormone levels over time when we have an acute episode of stress.

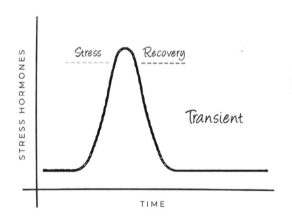

FIG 2. THE TRANSIENT STRESS RESPONSE.

We are designed to handle the acute episodes of stress that kick in when our brains feel like we are in danger or when we're being threatened. The stress hormones flood in immediately and enable us to fight or to flee the danger. This response is as old as the hills and gives us supernatural powers to help us survive.

This is why you can jump out of the way of an oncoming vehicle before you even think about it. This is what kicks in when people demonstrate supernatural strength by lifting cars off injured people in a crisis. Aren't our bodies amazing?

After an episode like that, you would probably suffer from shock and need some time to calm down. That's completely normal and is just our bodies recovering and bringing down the levels of stress hormones flying around.

That's what we are designed for, and it works like a dream without us having to think about it. It has meant that we have survived where other species haven't.

What we are not designed for is prolonged periods of stress. Periods when the stress hormones go up, but don't come down. With prolonged stress, the hormone levels remain elevated. Before we can recover from the last event, another stressful episode occurs and sets off the stress response, again and again and again.

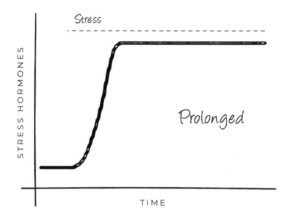

FIG 3. A PROLONGED STRESS RESPONSE.

We don't really have any life-threatening things going on in the course of our everyday lives. But here's the thing: our brains don't know the difference between the threat of a bear about to chase us and the new deadline that has just been sprung upon us by a difficult boss.

Both events threaten us and trigger the stress response.

Our brains are continuously scanning for threats, and we seek comfort in certainty and knowing where we stand. When things change, it takes a while for the brain to feel safe. It scans around for potential dangers and does its best to create the safety and certainty that it needs to function at its best. If it doesn't feel safe, it will remain in the stress state and its functioning will be suboptimal.

Chronic stress is not good for you, but the trouble is that the chronic stressed feeling can start to be habitual after a while. It starts to feel normal. So many people these days have no sense of being in stress or when they are in the all-important recovery phase.

Without that knowledge, you can't possibly know whether you have the stress-versus-recovery ratio in balance. Fortunately, there is biofeedback technology that can show you what's happening on the inside. I use wearable biofeedback technology with all my one-to-one coaching clients as a vital tool to help them understand and shift their behaviour so that they get the balance right and are not continuously triggering the stress response and draining the battery. There's more about this in Chapter 7.

Stress hormones

What are stress hormones and what do they do?

When we are threatened, there is an immediate release of:

1. **Adrenaline**: increases our heart rate and blood pressure and gives us an immediate surge in energy. The prime purpose of this energy surge is to help us manage our dangerous situation by fighting or running away. This hormone is responsible for our immediate responses when we feel stressed. It helps us focus our attention on the matter in hand.

2. **Norepinephrine**: makes us feel more awake and responsive by shifting the blood flow to the areas that are likely to need it and away from areas that are less important. Blood flows towards the muscles and away from the skin.

And shortly afterwards, another hormone is released:

3. **Cortisol:** increases sugar in the bloodstream for energy and suppresses the processes that are not necessary, such as digestion, reproduction and immunity. None of these functions are necessary in a life-or-death situation.

Chronic stress – an extended period of time when the stress hormones flood the system – is not good for us, as these hormones suppress vital functions, as mentioned above. This can lead to digestive problems, heart disease, diabetes, reduced libido, acne, depression, back pain, weight gain and much more.

Stress has been shown to increase the likelihood of divorce and even to reduce our life expectancy. What I find fascinating is that these mechanisms are designed perfectly to ensure our survival and yet are backfiring all the time because of the crazy way we live our modern lives.

But that's not all; there is another hormone playing havoc, too. Dopamine is having a field day. It's designed to ensure we stay motivated so we can stay alive and pro-create – and it's highly addictive. These days, dopamine is driving us to seek out short-term pleasures that are not always good for us (e.g., incessantly checking our phones or anticipating a drink after work).

Communication model

We take in millions of bits of data every second. We couldn't possibly be conscious of them all because the information would overwhelm us, so our brain does an efficient job of simplifying things. It does this in several ways.

Firstly, it deletes, distorts and generalises information to make our life simpler.

It deletes information that we just don't need to know right now. For example, it has probably deleted your awareness of your left big toe, unless you are having a problem with it. But as soon as I suggested that thought, your brain probably stopped deleting and you could feel your toe.

Another way of simplifying the data coming in is by assigning meaning to it, which is another way of saying that we distort the data. Two people could see the same event and have all the same data coming in but could make two very different meanings. It's not that either meaning is wrong; they're just different.

The last way of simplifying all the millions of bits of information coming in is by generalising. For example, we don't have to think about how a door opens every time we see one. When we see hinges on one side and a handle on the other, we know from past experience how the door is likely to work.

Having simplified the data coming in, the brain then passes the information through a number of filters: our past history and memories, our beliefs and values, our past images, how things have felt in our physiology, and what our past language, both internal and external, has told us. All these things create the way we feel – our state – which then affects our decisions, our actions and finally the results we produce.

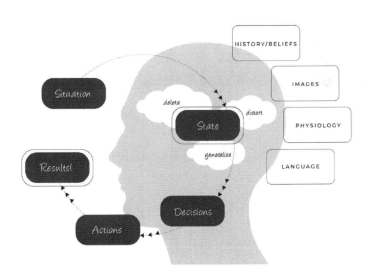

FIG 4. CAUSES AND EFFECTS OF MENTAL STATE.

Understanding this explains why others may see things so differently to you and make very different choices.

It follows that if you want to get different results in your life, you need to work backwards and change the way your brain processes and filters the data coming in so that you feel different, which will then enable different decisions, actions and results.

Brain facts

There are some other facts about the brain that I didn't know. I find that extraordinary, because I studied bio-chemistry and physiology at university– but back in the 80s, much of this probably wasn't widely known.

It's only relatively recently that we discovered the brain is elastic and that we can grow new neurons and make new connections. Back then, I believed every drunken evening was killing my brain cells, which I guess to some extent was true. But at least I now know it's not irrevocable.

If only I had also known about the brain's capacity and use of energy.

Energy

Brain work uses up lots of energy, and some things consume more energy than others. Prioritising, for example, takes the most effort and needs to be done when the brain has lots of capacity.

Decision-making is also energy-consuming. For brain optimisation, we need to be choosing between two things rather than many. It's one reason why Steve Jobs wore the same outfit to work every day.

Capacity

Our brain can only hold a certain amount of information in the prefrontal cortex (the bit of the brain we use to think). It's a much smaller 'stage' than people originally thought. The less you hold in your brain, the better. New concepts take up more space, so we need a clear head to start.

Our memory degrades as we try to hold more things in our prefrontal cortex.

Eventually, our prefrontal cortex gets full and stops being able to take in information. Taking some time out at that stage allows the brain to do vital processing. Even if you think you are not doing much, your brain is very busy. It decides what it needs to keep in the forefront of your mind, what it needs to store and put in the long-term memory bank, and what it can ditch. If you don't take time out, your brain will continue to function suboptimally.

I remember distinctly, during my accountancy exams, not being able to read an exam paper. My brain was full up and just not able to take in any more information. I had an urge to go for a walk and calm down, but I didn't request a loo break and kept trying to carry on. It didn't work. I failed that paper, even though it was one I had felt very confident about. It wasn't my intellect or memory that was the issue; it was my lack of understanding about how to get my brain to function at its best.

You can only focus on one thing at a time. Even if you think you are multitasking, you are in fact just switching between one task and another. This switching consumes lots of energy and results in more mistakes being made and things taking longer. If you continue to multitask, you'll experience a big drop-off in accuracy and performance. The only way to do two mental tasks quickly is to do one at a time. God, if only I had known that!

You've probably noticed that we humans are easily distracted – which makes sense if our brains are continuously scanning for threats or seeking pleasures. To focus, concentrate and do quality work, we need to eliminate distractions as much as possible (more about that later). Your brain always being 'on' can lower your IQ significantly.

Disconnecting from day-to-day challenges allows our brains to integrate and make new connections. That's why we can find insights popping into our brains when we are in the shower or just hanging loose. Our brains need downtime for integration and insight. If you don't allow your brain to have some time out, you cannot possibly function at your best.

I read recently that 50% of our working days are being used to just receive and manage information rather than using that information to do productive work. No wonder our brains are overwhelmed.

Brain health

Brain health isn't something most people consider when they are thinking about their health. People seem to think their bodies start from the neck down so, when they consider health, they don't spend much time thinking about what's going on above their shoulders.

That's crazy when we value our brain power and intellect over many other things.

The things I will share with you in the SELF section all help the brain to function at its best.

But what else does the brain need?

- **Sleep**: during sleep our brains are very busy. They flush out any debris that built up in the brain during the day; if this doesn't happen, the debris can build up and cause problems in the future. There is a strong link between dementia and the beta-amyloid that is built up during the day and flushed out at night. If you don't have sufficient sleep, your body and brain cannot do their best to keep you healthy. During sleep our brains also sort out the day's events and consolidate our memories. If you don't get enough sleep, you are negatively affecting your memory.

- **Stimulation**: our brains are elastic – they keep growing throughout our lives. Growing new neurons and neural pathways keeps us young and alive. Learning new things is a great way to build new neural pathways and promote genius. This is also true of hanging out with people who stimulate us and get us thinking.

- **Environment**: having an ordered environment also helps. Our brains take in millions of bits of sensory information every minute, and it's exhausting. Having a simple and uncluttered environment reduces brain stimulation and helps with its energy consumption.

- **Exercise**: improves our brain plasticity.

- **Squashing ANTS** (automatic negative thoughts): this is key for optimal brain function, and it's something you can read about in one of the blogs on my website.

- **Good nutrition and hydration**: I hope this goes without saying. Many doctors recommend supplements to also optimise brain health and function, but as I'm not an expert on that subject, I will leave it to you to do your research.

Busyness doesn't equal productivity

As far as I can remember, not once in all the time I spent in the Priory, or in the months and years of recovery afterwards, did anyone recommend exercise, sleep or downtime. But I now see these as essential to my mental wellbeing and productivity, and I won't compromise on them.

The rest of this book is dedicated to tools and tactics you can apply immediately to improve your current situation, with a focus on bringing down the stress hormones.

PART 2

CHAPTER 3

INTRODUCING THE STOP MODEL

*"Success is liking yourself, liking what you do,
and liking how you do it."*

MAYA ANGELOU

Have you met people who seem to be able to take their busy and demanding lives in their stride? They have demanding jobs, with lots of responsibility, but by and large they seem to stay on top of things.

Maybe you think they can't have the same level of demands on their time, the same sort of home life, the same boss that you have to battle with every day, the same systems or client demands and difficulties that you do.

The truth is that we just don't know what they have on their plate, but what I do know after more than 20 years in this field is that there are some people out there who are doing things differently.

They are not perfect. They don't get everything right. But what they can do is quickly get themselves back on track if they have fallen by the wayside.

What I have noticed about this group of individuals is that they are not unique and are not doing anything amazingly special. They haven't all been educated at the same schools or had 'good', stable upbringings. They are not the same age or gender. They are not all doing the same type of jobs – in fact, I have seen them in all walks of life – but there is something different about them.

It's not determination; I have seen plenty of people with determination who don't have a sustainable success strategy. In fact, many of them seem to have a determined strategy to self-destruct!

So if determination isn't the key, what is? There are three keys:

- **Awareness**: these people are aware of how they are feeling and therefore behaving. They are aware of the results they are getting and whether those are the results they want.

- **Clarity**: they have complete clarity about their desired outcome; they can picture it. It isn't some wishy-washy 'I'd like to have it someday', but a concrete idea of what they are working towards. The end result is clear to them, and although they take action every day towards their goals, they are not wedded to the 'how'. It's just that they keep their eye on the prize.

- **Lifelong learning**: you might call them 'lifelong learners' but they might not even recognise that in themselves. This group is not static but continues to grow in the many different aspects of their lives. They take on new challenges and constantly seek to grow.

The beginnings of a model

In my recovery period, I became curious about how I had succumbed to depression and anxiety when others didn't. Why couldn't I hack the pace when others seemed to be able to do so? What was I doing wrong? Or, more importantly, what were they doing right – and could I copy them?

That's how it all started. My curiosity was tweaked. The quest was on.

How the model developed

While my interest started in that period, it took me years to summarise my findings and finally get them into this book. The first thing I noticed about Thrivers is that they have found a way to bring out the best in themselves by being kind to their bodies and minds.

Personally, I broke through from a place of breakdown and, because of that, I have helped my clients move from a place of struggling to survive to a place of thriving today. I hope I can do the same for you.

Not only did the model I'm about to share with you work to get me back on track, but it has worked with hundreds of my clients over the years. Not every client has followed everything I have suggested; in fact, it works best when people pick and choose what is going to work for them.

Ruth and Jane's stories

Take **Ruth**. When I met Ruth, she described her job as 'wading through treacle'. Everything was hard work. She hated going to work in the mornings, dragging herself out of the house and commuting to work with a feeling of dread.

It took so much energy to leave her young daughter, and she was wondering whether it was all worth it. Was it worth giving up 'Mum time' for a job she loathed? She was ready to quit as she felt undervalued, not listened to, and miserable.

But the thing was, she didn't always loathe it. In fact, she used to love her job and feel excited about her contribution. What had changed?

Organisations change over time, with people coming and going, new management and new ideas. Ruth also acknowledged that she had changed, too.

We worked together and identified the biggest areas that were holding her back. I gave her some specific strategies from the Choose to Thrive model so she could feel more fulfilled in her job and working environment. Using these strategies, it didn't take long for her to change the way she felt.

Interesting, isn't it? The job didn't change, and nor did the people around her, but her attitude to her job and to others changed and she got a different result.

She is now more settled in her role and knows she is much more in control. Others are seeing the positive change in her, too, and she has been given more responsibility and recommended for promotion.

She now knows how she can change her experience, and is in the driving seat of her life. She's delighted she didn't quit but instead found the tools to turn her life around. As she said to me recently: 'I feel like a winner not a loser.'

Jane was so overwhelmed that, when she woke up in the morning, she would pull the covers over her head, just wanting to cry. After she had snoozed her alarm five times, she would have to do ten deep breaths just to get herself out of bed.

She would glance at her emails and then jump in the shower, already thinking about the day ahead. She went through the motions of getting breakfast for the kids while she was preoccupied with everything that was waiting for her at the office.

When she got to the office, she would find her desk strewn with little Post-it Notes covering everything she had to remember. She felt like she was drowning.

When I met Jane, she was just about to throw in the towel.

In our first session, she became aware of just how stressful and demanding her life was and what impact that was having on everything – her physiology, her mood and her ability to think straight, be a good mum and be a good leader.

We talked through the Choose to Thrive model and I gave her some specific strategies to focus on to get her back on track, so she could balance life and home. It took a while to implement the suggestions, but now she wakes up in the morning and is not worried about work but can instead enjoy being with her family.

She works as hard as ever, but now she feels productive and efficient, getting to the end of the day knowing she's done a good job and is making progress. She has told me that her life has completely turned around. She finally feels back in control and on top of things again.

How about you?

So how about you? Are you the person who gets reminders every day that your software needs updating and keeps pressing the 'remind me tomorrow' button? If you do that with your life, then nothing will change. But if you read and take action, taking a few small steps every day, you can expect your life to change for the better in a relatively short period of time.

Consequently, all sorts of things will be different. You'll feel better and more in control. Your interactions with others will be more purposeful and impactful, so you'll have more success at work and improved relationships at home.

What do they say? 'You can't pour from an empty cup.' Looking after number one will mean you have so much more energy for everything else. You'll be able to support others in your life, whether that is at home or at work.

The truth is that it all starts with you.

There is no magic bullet or pill that is going to make everything alright without you putting in some focused effort. Sorry about that. It will take some work on your part – but boy, will it be worth it.

I have broken down the steps into micro-steps, so that it doesn't feel overwhelming or insurmountable. What's more, you can start anywhere; choose the areas that sound like easy wins for you or things you will enjoy, and start there.

Take the exercises that work for you and let go of the rest. This is your life – no one else can do this for you or knows what is best for you. Not even your nearest and dearest. We are all different, and yet a combination of sensible, grounded steps will absolutely help you on your way.

Let's do this!

By all means, if you feel you need more help understanding and implementing the model, do sign up for some coaching support, which you can do on my website: **www.sarahsparks.co.uk**

Choose to Thrive

So what are the key components of the Choose to Thrive model?

FIG 5. THE CHOOSE TO THRIVE (STOP) MODEL.

Self

Thrivers know how important it is to look after themselves and know where they are going.

If you don't look after yourself and have a strong sense of who *you* are, then you can find yourself on a path dictated by others, which leads to low self-esteem, a lack of confidence, and feeling not good enough, unhappy and unfulfilled – essentially feeling compromised, living someone else's dream.

What I'm going to teach is how to boost your energy levels and set your inner compass so you can get back in the driving seat and feel more in control, feeling aligned and living the life you want.

Time

Thrivers know that time is a limited resource and that every moment matters. Thrivers focus on using their time to get the best results and don't confuse busyness with productivity.

If you don't master how you use time, you can find yourself caught in the 'busy trap', running to keep up but wondering what you have achieved by the end of the day.

What I'm going to teach is how to increase your productivity, stay focused and buy yourself some time so you can achieve more and worry less.

Others

Thrivers know how important relationships with others are to their success. They have mastered how to have impact and influence and build effective relationships that work.

If you don't manage your relationships effectively, interacting with others can be hard work and ineffective, resulting in stressful situations and stalled careers.

What I'm going to teach is how to build relationships that work and take the stress out of interacting with others.

Performance

Thrivers know that if they want a successful career, they need to have their long-term performance in the front of their mind.

If you don't focus on your long-term performance, you're likely to give all you've got only to crash and burn at a later stage, sacrificing your career, relationships, health and wellbeing along the way.

What I'm going to teach is how to make better choices that have your long-term sustainable performance in mind, so you can reap the rewards over the years and set yourself up for long-term success.

As one of my clients, Helen, said: 'Working with Sarah has had a positive impact in all aspects of my life – from my career to my relationship with my husband and even my relationship with my parents.'

"The future depends on what you do today."

MAHATMA GANDHI

You can do this!

I know that you are short of time and want results, which is why this book is full of strategies, easy tips and exercises that don't take long to do and yet can have a profound impact on how you feel and your productivity.

I have split the exercises into:

- **SURVIVE toolkit**: quick and dirty exercises that you could do right away. These are for when you have limited time but need a shift.

- **THRIVE toolkit**: more in-depth exercises that require more time but build the strong foundations you need for future success.

If you have time, after each exercise apply the 'WWW. EBI' principle. Ask yourself 'What Worked Well' and what would be 'Even Better If'. This is a gentle way to give yourself feedback and encourage yourself to grow.

Grab your new journal or the workbook from my website, and let's get started: **www.sarahsparks.co.uk/ideas/download-your-workbook-here/**

It's good to have all the exercises in one place for future reference and to remind yourself of just how far you've come.

Remember, tomorrow never comes – you have to act now. Even the smallest step will make a difference.

OK. Let's go.

SELF

"Where you are is the result of who you were, but where you go, depends entirely on who you choose to be."

HAL ELROD

What is the SELF step all about?

Understanding yourself is the first step towards being able to thrive. It's the foundation that will set you up for future success.

But what do I mean by 'understanding yourself'?

It's understanding your energy and knowing how to boost it if the batteries are low. It's understanding your mood and considering whether it is serving you right now – and if not, what you should do about it.

It's the things that you've probably thought about but are not doing consistently or perhaps have never explored. It's the understanding of where you are, and where you want to go – or of what's important to you and why certain things bring you joy while other things drive you mad.

In this chapter I'll be helping you boost your energy and mood, identify your values and decide your future direction so that you will be able to cope more easily with today's demands and know you are on your chosen path.

Why is the SELF step important?

Do you frequently run around trying to please other people? Do you do what is requested of you without questioning it? Maybe you're trying to be 'Super Career Person' or 'Super Mum (or Dad)'. You might be doing a pretty good job, but the effort is wearing and incessant.

Maybe you have lost your rudder and have no idea what direction you want to be travelling in. Unless someone else was setting the destination, you'd probably just sit still. Sound familiar?

The thing is, when you're so busy doing things for other people it's easy to miss the fact that you're not at the wheel. Because you are moving forward, it feels like you're getting somewhere. But where are you going? If you don't know, or you do know and it's not somewhere you want to go, then life can become a struggle – one you're not winning!

Once you know who you are and what you want, life is so much simpler and less stressful. You don't pursue things unless they bring you joy, satisfaction and success.

So many of the choices melt away. That prevents feelings of being overwhelmed and instead promotes joy.

What happens when you overlook SELF?

Personal story - someone else's dream

When I was about to leave university, I didn't have a clue what I wanted to do. I had studied biochemistry and physiology, which was not my first choice; I had wanted to be a doctor, but my school's headmistress said I wouldn't get in and shouldn't bother trying! I believed her and let go of the wheel.

When it came to deciding what to do after university, I had a chat with my dad. He thought I should do accountancy, because it would give me a good grounding in business and would always be needed by others, anywhere in the world.

He was right about that, but neither of us considered whether it was really going to bring out the best in me. Dad did a bit of research and sent me a handwritten note that I have hidden somewhere to this day. It had a list of four accountancy firms on it. Next to one of them, Arthur Andersen, he had written, 'They are the best and you'll never get in.'

My dad was a good man, but he hadn't achieved everything he wanted in life. Although he was an MD of a company, he never completed his accountancy exams, and regretted it. Looking back, I suspect that his recommendation probably said more about what he wanted to do rather than what I wanted to do.

But he did know that if I was ever set a challenge I would step up and give it my best shot. That's exactly what I did, and I joined Arthur Andersen in June 1982 on the princely wage of £5,400 pa. It felt like an enormous amount of money back then and was more than any other accountancy firm was paying. I was proud of myself but had no clue I was following someone else's dream and setting off along a path that would have profound implications.

Have you ever found yourself doing that? It could be small things like when someone asks, 'Where shall we go for dinner?' and your usual response is, 'Oh I don't mind. You choose.' However, deep down, you know you have hidden your preference to make life easier.

Or perhaps after a long and exhausting day at work, you know you should go home and recover, but others persuade you to go for a drink (which leads to many) and instead of saying no, you fall in line. If you are not careful, you can wake up years later realising you haven't been at the steering wheel of your life and finding yourself somewhere you don't want to be.

It's OK to go after what you want, as long as it is what you really, really want! If you do, you'll more than likely thrive and fulfil your potential– but if you don't, you'll be compromising yourself, and that automatically puts you in the stress response.

Do that for a lifetime and it's no wonder people end up miserable, sick and tired. It's your duty to be your best self so that you can fulfil your potential and be the best for others. It's like the oxygen mask metaphor: if you fit your own oxygen mask first, others will get the best of you not the rest of you.

Let's start by taking a look at your energy and mood.

Step 1: Boosting your energy!

What's your energy doing?

When was the last time you charged your phone? Chances are it was within the last 24 hours. You do it automatically, right? And if you don't, your phone will run out of charge and be useless, and then you'll feel like you lost a limb!

But when was the last time you checked in on your own energy levels? How charged is *your* battery right now? Has it been depleting recently, or have you managed to keep it topped up to the max?

Most people don't even think about their own energy and battery levels. They keep going, pushing through, and wondering why over time they are feeling exhausted and not functioning at their best. But even that often doesn't seem to be a wake-up call. They start normalising these feelings and just keep on draining the battery.

It doesn't work. Whether you are young, old, super fit or sluggish, resilient or not resilient, you can't keep draining the battery and expect to get away with it. Eventually your body will give you feedback.

There will be aches, pains, tummy trouble, headaches, skin conditions and all the rest of it, and if you continue to ignore these messages, you will shut down. If you ignore it, your body *will* take things into its own hands and do the only thing it can to survive.

That's what happened to me and resulted in my rocking to and fro in a mental hospital, not being able to take in the easiest of instructions or do a simple jigsaw.

Looking after yourself and your energy is key to mastering your Self.

You can't avoid it. If you really want to feel good, get joy and satisfaction from your life, and have a successful career, you have to look after your energy. Period.

So how do you do that? We are complex organisms; not all things work for all people when it comes to energising yourself. However, there are some basic principles and must do's that are common to all of us humans.

"There've been many times that I haven't noticed I'm starting to burn out, often because it's been at the peak times of my career when everything has looked like it's going great on the outside. I might have been getting promoted, taking on bigger roles, my profile was increasing, but on the inside, I was slowly breaking. I can keep going like this for a couple of years, but I think there's micro-burnouts the whole way along before I become completely exhausted. Over time, I've learnt that having good boundaries in place is the key."

MID-THIRTIES WOMAN WORKING FOR AN INTERNATIONAL BANK

Sleep

In my opinion, sleep is the most underrated health habit, the best productivity- and happiness-enhancing behaviour there is. We all know this… when we care to stop and think about it.

If you've been lucky enough to experience a long-haul flight, you know how jaded you felt when you landed; you probably couldn't wait for the day to be over so you could get to bed. The last thing you want to be doing that day is making important decisions, as your brain feels like mush.

You could probably manage mundane tasks like unpacking your suitcase, but anything creative, that requires problem-solving or complex thinking, is just going to have to wait until another day. You might even be short tempered with others or have a lower mood.

And yet on a day when you've had a good night's sleep, you feel amazing. Nothing seems to faze you. You get through so much stuff, do your exercise routine and choose a healthy option for lunch. Ideas seem to spring out of nowhere and it's easy to think clearly and get important decisions made. It's a completely different experience.

Research has shown time and time again that sleep is vital for our wellbeing. Harvard Medical School talks about how sleep deprivation negatively impacts our moods, our ability to focus and our ability to access high cognitive function.

While we sleep, important functions are going on that can't happen in the same way if we short-change ourselves. During those vital hours of shut-eye, our thoughts are organised and put down in our memory bank. Vital cleansing of the brain takes place, clearing out harmful proteins like beta-amyloid, which is linked to dementia.

The quality of our day and our mood improves with good sleep, and we're able to deal with our day-to-day challenges so much more effectively.

Have you found that when you don't have enough sleep, things take longer to do? For me it feels like wading through treacle. I completely slow down, find it so much more difficult to take in information and I make way more mistakes. How many people do you know who are not getting enough sleep? Just imagine the cumulative consequences of this sleep-deprived brain fog.

But how much is enough? Well, according to The Sleep Foundation, if you're an adult between the ages of 18 and 64 you need seven to nine hours of sleep a night.[16] Very few adults can get away with less. They may boast about being able to get by on five or six hours, but it's simply not true.

Around the world many people are compromising on their sleep. Let's hope the leaders of these countries are not included in the statistics!

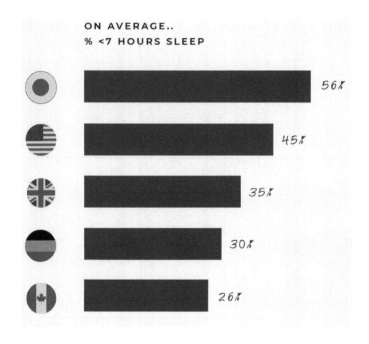

ON AVERAGE..
% <7 HOURS SLEEP

56%

45%

35%

30%

26%

FIG 6. SLEEP HOURS BY NATION.[17]

Unfortunately, sleep deprivation starts to feel normal after a while – ask any new mum! – even though our effectiveness diminishes significantly.

There have been a number of studies about this over the years, but one by Van Dongen et al in 2003 showed very clearly that, although participants knew they were being sleep deprived, they did not perceive that this deprivation was negatively affecting their performance.[18]

As mentioned, I used to think that sleep was a waste of time, and completely overrated. I thought long hours in bed were for lazy people and sleep was something I could do without. How wrong I was. I can't bear to think of the damage I might have caused myself from my ignorant and immature attitude.

So, what about you? How much sleep are you getting? Are you getting enough or are you compromising on sleep to get things done?

I'm sure you have seen young children when they reach the end of their sleep quota. They go from happily playing to a full-blown meltdown, and we know that things are not going to improve for them unless they go and get some sleep.

Well, I'm sorry to be the bearer of bad news, but the same is true of adults.

We run out of energy and need to get some sleep. We might be able to control our meltdown more effectively than a young child, but the same things are going on inside: reduced emotional control, an inability to think straight or be rational, and the fact that we will continue to make mistakes and take longer to do things until we catch up.

There is no way of avoiding it. We humans need our sleep.

**SURVIVE toolkit exercise:
sleep monitoring**

For the next week I'd like you to monitor your sleep. If you have a smart watch or Fitbit, these gadgets will do it for you. But even if you don't have one of these devices, I want you to keep a track of the hours of sleep you are getting and write it in your journal. Don't cheat! The only person who will see this is you, so you will only be cheating yourself.

In your journal, write down:

- The time you went to bed

- The time you got up

- Hours of sleep

Things that might have interrupted or helped your sleep (e.g. arguments, workload, hot bath).

At the end of the week, review what this information is telling you. Are you getting enough sleep, or do you need to start thinking about how you can get more? There are plenty of recommendations about what you can do to improve your sleep on the internet. The Sleep Foundation is a good place to look: **www.sleepfoundation.org**.

I now protect my sleep like a hawk, and I don't allow myself or others to steal it from me.

Hydration

I used to be a coffee girl, having at least 10 cups of coffee a day. Yes, I know that sounds a lot, but I loved it; it made me feel energised, and boy, did I need that pick-me-up most days! I didn't drink much water. It was coffee during the day to lift me up, and wine in the evenings to calm me down. Sounds great – or so I thought.

I had no idea that even the smallest amount of dehydration negatively affects our concentration. Did you?

And, of course, my beverages of choice were diuretics, meaning that they sucked water out of me. I was peeing out more liquid than I was taking in.

Now, if you think about the fact that our bodies on average are made up of 60% water, and that every single system within the body relies on hydration to function well and flush out toxins, it's no surprise that drinking enough water every day is essential.

What the hell was I doing? Why was I making things so difficult for myself?

Now I know more, hydration is something I really focus on and keep topped up. Let me share a few facts.

How much water is enough every day? The answer is… it depends. A variety of factors come into play: whether you live in a hot climate, whether you are typically a sweaty person, how much physical exercise you do, what you've been eating, what else you are drinking, and so on.

But don't let this bamboozle you. The chances are you are not drinking enough water. Period.

How can you tell? You get feedback every time you go to the loo! If your pee is dark and smelly (sorry to be rather basic here), you are dehydrated and need to drink more water. If your pee is a light straw colour and doesn't smell, then you're probably OK.

If you've just gone to the loo to check it out and you real-ise that you need to top up the water quota, don't just gulp a glass of water down in one go; ideally, sip it.

Why is that? Well, think about it: the cells throughout your body are gasping for more hydration but they can't just soak it up instantaneously from your stomach. The blood has to distribute it around the body– but, in the mean-time, the kidneys have detected an excess of water in the system and do their best to bring back the balance by creating urine.

So it's much better to drink small amounts of water throughout the day rather than large quantities when you are dehydrated and feel thirsty. By the way, the thirst feed-back loop is a pretty slow one, so by the time you feel thirsty you are well and truly dehydrated.

Having said that, drinking more water is better than drinking less. Aim for about two litres a day. One of the best ways to achieve that is to fill a two-litre bottle in the morning and make sure it's empty by the end of the day.

What triggers could you set up to remind you to treasure your body and drink the water it vitally needs? Maybe set an alarm to go off every half an hour, or have a drink of water every time you get up to go to the loo, or the kitchen, or for a walk around the office/house?

Once it's a habit, it's a habit and your body will really thank you for drinking the water you need every day.

Nutrition

I need to make something clear here before I start. I am not a nutritionist, and I am not advocating any sort of diet.

But what I do want to highlight in this section are some obvious things that many in this fast-paced, crazy world are either ignoring or just don't know. As Eric Edmeades, the founder of Wildfit, says: 'It's not your fault.' We've never been taught this stuff, and the food industry does its very best to keep us in this naïve state.

By the way, I highly recommend you look Eric up, and if you get tempted to do his Wildfit programme, then do it – it will change your relationship to food and your life forever!

I approach nutrition from a very basic level with some simple principles in mind:

- Was I born and designed to eat this stuff?

- How processed is it? (i.e., how much has the food been interfered with to get it to my table?)

- Is it providing the essential ingredients my body needs?

- Am I fuelling my body at appropriate times during the day?

Don't get me wrong; I haven't always eaten and thought this way, but I do now I know how nutrition affects my mood and energy.

Like many city professionals, I would leave home at the crack of dawn on an empty stomach and drink coffee through the morning. I would grab something sugary around 11, then skip lunch or rush down to the canteen for a sandwich. Then it would be more coffee when I started flagging in the afternoon.

Looking back, within those 12-plus hours at work, I put hardly anything in my body that was actually helping me thrive.

I don't know about you, but I reckon our bodies are awesome. Whatever is going on in our worlds, our bodies do their very best to keep going and support us every step of the way. They are pretty sophisticated machines. Most of the complex systems and processes go on completely without our awareness, until something begins not to work as it should.

Now ponder this: if you owned a Ferrari, would you put premium fuel into it to maximise its performance or would you put in the cheapest fuel you could find, compromising its performance and probably causing internal damage?

The same is true of our sophisticated machines. We shouldn't be putting cheap crap fuel into them, like take-aways and ready meals. It makes no sense if you want to give your body a chance to do its magic well.

So what *should* you do?

Firstly, be aware of what you are doing now. Are you skip-ping meals? Are you having sugar in every meal? Even if you think not, check the ingredients – you may find out otherwise.

Sugar is addictive, and food producers know it. You have to be very discerning to really eliminate sugar from your diet. Seriously– go check it. Even cooked prawns or ham have sugar in them. Once you start noticing what the food industry is doing, it may well enrage you. It certainly did me.

Let me get off the soapbox for a minute so we can think logically. What did our ancestors eat? They foraged for plant-based food most of the time, and then occasionally would have had large doses of protein when they caught a fish or animal. Everything was fresh, seasonal and clean.

Now, I know that's not easy to do, but you find cultures around the world who eat more akin to this, and you'll often find that people who belong to these same cultures live a long and healthy life too.

I don't recommend any particular diet, but the research I have done suggests that the Mediterranean diet is a good one to follow for your brain, mood and health. Unlike junk food, which is linked to heart disease, diabetes and weight gain, a Mediterranean diet is linked to healthy longevity.

What is a Mediterranean diet? Lots of fresh fruit and veg-etables, plenty of fish, some meat, nuts, olive oil, red wine (yes, red wine), coffee and plain chocolate (yes, that's on the list too). Doesn't sound too bad, does it?

Currently, as I write this chapter, I am feeling hungover and out of sorts. It's not something I'm proud to admit, bearing in mind what I preach; however, I am one for shar-ing, warts and all.

Last night I met up with a long-standing friend. We hadn't seen each other for about six months and wanted to treat ourselves to a night out at a special restaurant. We decided to eat out at a lovely fish restaurant on the Thames. All sounds good so far.

The reality turned out to be something else. Instead of treating ourselves, we treated ourselves badly. The starters and main courses we chose were in line with the Mediterranean diet but, after half a bottle of champagne each, our discerning faculties flew out the window and we decided to have more bubbly and a dessert.

I feel crap this morning. My body is screaming at me, 'Why did you do that?' I certainly wish now that I'd said no to the extra glass and that massive sugar hit before bedtime. I couldn't sleep, my food wouldn't go down, I felt slightly sick but not enough to be so. All in all, I really had abused my sophisticated machine, and it was complaining.

Won't be doing that again in a hurry. Off to have a green smoothie!

Don't get me wrong; it's absolutely fine to have a blowout from time to time, but the message I want to share here is – be conscious and choose what you are doing. If you want or need to get up the next morning and thrive – then think about what you need to do to really 'treat yourself'.

THRIVE toolkit exercise:
nutrition

Grab your journal and let's go.

Assuming it's likely to be a pretty typical day, over the next 24 hours I want you to write down everything that goes into your awesome body. Remember, no one else is going to see this, so you could lie and not write everything down – but you're going to find this exercise invaluable if you are honest with yourself.

Before you start, I want you to think about *nutrition* instead of 'good' or 'bad' food.

Looking at everything you have put in your mouth in the last 24 hours, what do you notice?

1. What did you eat?

2. When did you eat? Are you eating regularly during the day? Do you snack?

3. How did you eat? On the go, sitting at a table, in a hurry, leisurely?

4. Do you think your body would thrive if this happened every day?

5.   What alternative foods could you consider?

6.   Are there better ways of spacing out your meals?

7.   How could you make these meals easier for your body to digest?

Nutrition top tips

Eat when you're hungry, not ravenous. Protein lasts longer than carbohydrate, so have some protein at every meal. Eat slowly and stop when you're 80% full.

Ask yourself these questions:

- How is this food made? Is it processed or natural? What's in it (or not in it)?

- Do I know what all these ingredients are?

- How does this food affect my body? How do I feel physically after eating it?

- Does this food, fundamentally, nourish me? Does it add or subtract value?

- What's an alternative to this food?

- Is this the best available choice under the circumstances?

SURVIVE toolkit exercise: nutrition

You might feel you can't spare the time right now to make a note of everything you're eating. I get it. I've been there.

Don't fret. Awareness is the first step in any change process, so if you don't have much time, do this instead: every time you put something in your mouth, just note it in your mind. Oh, that's a croissant. Or that's a beer and a pizza. No need to do any more than that. Stay away from any judgement and if you hear yourself being critical, just say to yourself instead, 'That's fascinating.' You might find by just doing this simple, quick awareness exercise that you start making different choices.

Movement

Most people in the western world know they need to move more, but it doesn't happen. You have good intentions, and then something else gets in the way, even though you know you feel so much better when you have exercised. You feel more alive, energised, vital – righteous, even. You look better and feel better. And there is so much evidence out there that it is good for our brains, building new neural pathways and longevity.

What happens when you don't exercise? For me, I feel sluggish and lethargic, have a self-loathing that I don't like admitting to, and I know I am saving up more problems for the future, not just physical but mental too. Did you know that you increase your risk of dementia if you don't move?

When I worked for Goldman, there was a gym at the office, but I went there maybe half a dozen times in all the years I was there. When I was working flat out, I didn't feel I had the time to do it, and my body and brain paid the price. Big time. My attitude now is that I don't have time *not* to exercise.

Why does exercise feel good when we do it? Well, it's because our body releases endorphins, those feel-good hormones.

Exercise strengthens our muscles, including our heart. Muscles quickly wither away when we don't use them; we lose 1–3% of muscle mass per *day* when bedridden. It's one of those potentially disheartening realisations that tells us there can be no let-up; we are going to have to keep exercising and moving for the rest of our lives if we want to keep our muscles strong. Gulp!

But exercise has another benefit too. When you're moving and engaged in the exercise you are doing, it's a great distraction from worry and stress. Research has shown that people who exercise are less likely to suffer from anxiety and depression, and scans can show that exercise increases brain connections and cognitive function and staves off cognitive decline.

In some research I did in 2016, 76% of participants acknowledged that exercise would improve their effectiveness, but only 33% felt they were doing enough.

For those of you who have never found exercise easy to do or to fit into a busy life, I get it. But if we can reframe our mindset to think about movement rather than 'exercise', I think it helps.

According to an article published by Harvard Health in 2014, exercise changes the brain in ways that protect memory and thinking skills. It said: 'In a study done at the University of British Columbia, researchers found that regular aerobic exercise, the kind that gets your heart and your sweat glands pumping, appears to boost the size of the hippocampus, the brain area involved in verbal memory and learning.'[19]

So are you moving your body enough?

Is the level of exercise or movement you're doing serving you right now, in terms of energy? Is it enough to benefit you in the long term? If the answer is no, then what could you do to get more movement into your life?

- Perhaps you could walk or cycle to the shops or your place of work instead of driving or taking the bus. Or, if you walk or cycle already, could you take a longer route?

- What about finding an accountability buddy? Is there someone you could move with?

- What about enjoyable moving? You don't have to stick to conventions here. You could join a dance class or a hiking club.

- What about using technology to set a goal and track your progress? There are many apps you could use for this. As they say, 'What gets measured gets done'.

If you haven't done much exercise recently, don't go mad. Take it easy to begin with – just do a few minutes a day at first, build it up over time, and see how your wellbeing improves.

I have always been a busy person, but I hadn't ever done much exercise until recently. When I got divorced, I went to a weekly dance class, which I discovered I loved. During the pandemic, I committed to moving my body every day and now I go for a cycle ride, take a long brisk walk, or do an online exercise class. There are so many possibilities to choose from.

For me, if I set my intention and make sure I do it before anything else in the day, then it gets done!

When I was really unwell, I was housebound. I have no idea what I did with my days as I can't remember, but I recall many occasions sitting at the breakfast table just staring out of the window aimlessly. The thought of getting out of the house never crossed my mind, other than to do the food shopping to keep us alive. And I found even that overwhelming.

The courage it took to cross the road was immense. There was just too much information bombarding me to be able to make sense of what I was seeing. I could not compute the speed of the traffic, the time I would need to cross the road safely, the sounds and the noise. I literally was like a rabbit in the headlights: paralysed and not knowing which way to turn.

And then when I was in the supermarket, the sensory noise of all the colour, choices, bustle and sounds was overwhelming. I just grabbed the nearest things and got out of there.

'What has this got to do with exercise?' I hear you ask.

Here's the thing: if only I had known then what I know now. If only my psychiatrist and doctors had insisted on me getting exercise. I don't remember them ever saying that exercise should be part of my recovery routine. Not once. To be fair, perhaps someone may have said something, but if they did, I just didn't take it in.

What I know now is that if I move more, I am less likely to find depression creeping back in.

I only discovered that because I read something about running increasing neurogenesis– brain growth. I want to do anything and everything that might reverse the damage I believe I did to my brain during those years of chronic stress. (By the way, weight training also increases neurogenesis. Not sure how or why, but it does.)

It's a scary thought that those years and years of working long hours and pushing myself way past what was good for me killed off some of my brain cells.

I now know that doing exercise (particularly running) makes me feel good and staves off depression. At this point of writing, I run for 15–30 mins three times a week. Not every week, but often.

The stats show that a larger and larger percentage of the population are becoming sedentary, commuting in their cars, having a desk-bound job, watching TV or fiddling with gadgets.

I met a man only yesterday who was really struggling to get up and down stairs. He looked my age (late fifties) and was slim. He admitted that there was nothing wrong with him, but said he was just getting old. It looked like he needed some oil in his joints.

He looked as though he didn't go up and down stairs very often, like his muscles and joints were creaking and struggling at the thought. But, you see, it's a bit like doing the crossword or sudoku. Use it or lose it. If you do something small every day, you are oiling the whole system.

Assuming nothing is wrong, I bet that young (in my mind) man could scamper up and down stairs if he got back into the routine of doing it every day.

Apart from helping to maintain a healthy body weight and reducing the risk of heart disease and diabetes, exercise may be the best mood and energy booster there is, and staves off anxiety and depression.

But it needs to be done consistently. It's better to do something for 20 minutes five times a week, every week, than to do two and a half hours of exercise once a week and nothing for a month.

According to the Alzheimer's Society, many studies show that regular exercise can significantly reduce the risk of developing dementia.[20]

SURVIVE toolkit exercise:
moving your body

If you don't have much (or any) time to move or exercise right now, do this instead. It can take less than a minute. Essentially, you want to move your body in every direction to increase mobility and flexibility, and get the blood moving.

Ideally you want to repeat these a few times:

- From a standing position, do a roll down towards your toes and return to the upright position.

- Raise your hands above your head and stretch gently (not too far) back.

- With one arm over your head and the other on your waist, reach towards the opposite side, then repeat on the other side.

- Standing tall, twist your body gently to one side and then the other.

That's it! That's all you need to do for now.

Breathing

Clearly, we have to breathe to stay alive. If you're reading this book, then you must be breathing, right? What else is there to know about breathing? And why is breathing *properly* so important?

When I was born there was a lot of stress in my household, as my elder sister was ill and not expected to live. I can't imagine the levels of stress that my mum and dad must have been going through as young new parents.

I suspect I must have picked up on that stress and embodied it. For the first 32 years of my life, I had eczema on my arms, legs and face – and it wasn't until I was taught how to breathe properly that it went away.

When we are under threat, whether it's perceived or real, our bodies kick off the stress response with all the associated chemical releases. One of the outputs is an increased pace of breathing to move oxygen to the muscles and away from anything that doesn't need it for the flight, fight or freeze response.

What if that hyperventilation just keeps happening because the body has stayed in its stress response? I don't know the answer from a medical perspective, but my suspicion is that this is what was happening to me.

I believe my body was permanently in a state of stress, and it was causing my skin to react.

When I was taught to breathe properly, my eczema disappeared overnight and has never returned. Finally, my body was able to relax and be in recovery mode most of the time.

I have subsequently taught a number of my clients with eczema how to breathe, and their skin too has miraculously improved. I am not professing to be any sort of expert here; I am only sharing what has worked for me and some of my clients.

If you have any sort of skin condition, it's worth giving it a go; I'll tell you how in a minute. Breathing properly takes our body out of the stress response.

It's one of the best ways I know to move from feeling stressed and frazzled to a place of calm and clarity in a matter of a few minutes. Don't take my word for it. Give it a go yourself.

SURVIVE toolkit exercise:
breathing properly

I recommend box breathing, a technique taught to the US Navy Sea, Air, and Land Teams (commonly known as Navy SEALs) to keep them calm under intense pressure. It's quite simple and I'd like you to give it a go right now. Yes– now.

It doesn't take long— less than a minute if that's all you have time for right now— but it is a technique you can use at any time to calm yourself down from a stressful situation. The other thing I really like about this technique is that no one needs to know you are doing it.

Grab your journal or a piece of paper and let's do it!

First of all, write down how stressed you're feeling— a score out of 10, where 10 is super stressed and one is cool, calm and almost horizontal.

Now breathe in for a count of four, hold it for four, breathe out for four, pause for four. Look to do this at least three times.

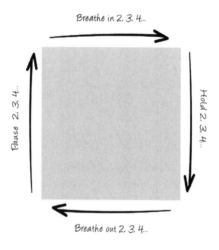

FIG 7. BOX BREATHING.

Now take a note of what's different.

Maybe you have a greater sense of calm, maybe you can detect that your heartbeat has decreased, or possibly that you have more clarity. Whatever it is, write it in the journal and give yourself another score out of 10 on the stress scale.

The chances are that your score has come down and that you're feeling calmer and more relaxed.

Answer the following questions in your journal:

- On a scale of 1–10, how useful was this exercise?

- Where could you use it in the future?

- Are there particular interactions that it would be good for you to do before you start?

- What meetings would this method be helpful in?

- Who else needs to know how to do this technique? Maybe your partner, friend, colleague, children…

- How will you share this information?

Managing your state

Are you in a state? Here's how to recognise it and what to do about it.

Most people think that being in a state is a negative thing, but the reality is that we are all in a state, all of the time. We can't not be.

For example, we're in a state of joy, of happiness, of anger, of frustration; we move in and out of these different states all the time.

Each state comes with its own set of related behaviours/ actions. You take different actions at work when you are feeling happy and refreshed than the actions you'd take when you are stressed, overwhelmed or tired. One state sees opportunities and possibilities, the other sees threats and hard work.

The question is: is your current state serving you?

If it's not, then you need to change it! It's as simple as that, and I'm not kidding. It is simple but maybe not always easy to get out of the negative state you are in, but what I want you to do is just acknowledge that you are always in a state and that it is possible to move from one state to another.

Sometimes a particular negative state is a bit of habit. It was for me.

I was in a grump for years! I didn't realise I had any control over my state and certainly didn't consciously know how to change it. When I discovered that it was possible, I started to experiment… and these days I can pretty much choose my state at will.

And it's so much better to choose your state at the beginning of the day rather than let it be dictated to you by events. I choose my state as part of my usual routine in the morning – but more of that later.

SURVIVE toolkit exercise:
changing your state

In this short exercise I will show you how to move from a negative unresourceful state in a matter of minutes. If you are feeling sceptical, all I can say is that you should give this a go! You won't know unless you try – and no, it won't work if you just read about it. You have to do it! Are you ready?

- I'd like you to stand up. Yes, wherever you are, you need to stand up. You can't do this sitting down, and it's not a spectator sport – so if you need to find yourself a quiet corner or wait until you are in the privacy of your own space then please do.

- Now recall a time or event that caused you distress or sadness. While you're connecting with this sad emotion, I want you to look up, put your shoulders back, stand tall, throw your arms in the air and say YES, YES, YES in a loud and determined voice.

- Keep going, saying YES, YES, YES, standing tall with your arms in the air, until you can no longer connect with your old emotional state. (Now you know why you needed to find a private space!)

- Notice how difficult it was to stay in the negative state. Now, you're probably feeling quite different.

Now that you have changed out of your negative state into something lighter, it should have proved to you that you can indeed move from state to state at will. You might have even found yourself laughing.

THRIVE toolkit exercise:
changing your state

If you have a little more time, jot down in your journal the answers to the following questions:

- How long did it take you to move out of your negative state?

- What states do you get yourself into, at work or at home, that don't serve you (e.g., overwhelm, anxiety, frustration, anger, fear)?

- Now that you have a list of unhelpful states, write down next to each one the state you would like to be in instead (e.g., calm instead of overwhelm, control instead of anxiety, confidence instead of frustration). You decide what feels right for you.

- Next, practise and connect with these more helpful states. So, while standing, connect with the positive emotional states and really step into how they feel. You might want to close your eyes and remind yourself of a time when you felt this way. The more you practise, the easier you will find it to shift to this more positive state.

The next time you find yourself in an unhelpful state, take yourself off somewhere – even the loo will do – and look up, put your shoulders back, stand tall, throw your arms in the air and say YES, YES, YES in a loud and determined voice.

Once you have got yourself out of the old state, pause and say, 'I choose to be in an (X) state instead' – where X is the resourceful state of confidence, calm, being in control, or whatever other positive state will help. Keep stepping into this positive-feeling emotional state until you are ready to face the world again.

Please make a note in your journal. What have you learnt from this exercise? And what will you do when you next find yourself in a negative state?

Here's another thought. Why wait until you're in a negative state? Why not be much more proactive and choose one that is going to serve you before your day starts? What state do you need to be in to have a good day today?

It may be a state of curiosity, or assertiveness, or strength, or kindness, or joy. You can choose. You have been in these states before and you can probably remember an event where you felt like that. And that's the trick.

Decide what state you want, write it down, recall a time when you experienced that state, try it on for size right away – really try it on and experience the feelings, thoughts and bodily sensations – and you're there.

You might find that your unwanted state comes back from time to time. That's OK; it probably means you're in a bit of a habit with that state and frequent it often.

It's not the end of the world, but it might require a bit more effort to continuously choose the state you want to be in. Keep going! It's such a great skill to have, to be able to choose your state. When you choose your state, you can choose a completely different life.

Now you have some tools to boost your energy, let's get started with some more exploring.

Step 2: Groundwork – who are you?

Where are you now?

Would you agree that you can't really set sail to a new destination unless you know where you are now? If so, how do you take stock of where you are? There are plenty of tools for this, but the one my clients find easiest to do is the wheel of life. It's quick, easy and can be done any time you want to take stock or remind yourself of how far you have come.

**THRIVE toolkit exercise:
wheel of life**

This quick exercise will give you an overview of where you are in your life right now, in relation to some of the most important aspects of your life.

1. Take out your new journal or a piece of paper and draw the largest circle you can.

2. Divide this circle into eight segments.

3. Label the segments as per the diagram below.

4. Value each of the wedges: taking the centre of the wheel as 0 and the outer edge as 10, rank your level by drawing a straight or curved line to create a new outer edge (see example below).

The values refer to how satisfied *you* are with this aspect of your life. This is not what other people, family, spouse, friends, or the world at large might think about the different areas of your life. This is just your own assessment, so be honest.

You may choose to relabel some of the wedges or split them differently. It's the wheel of *your* life, so you can decide.

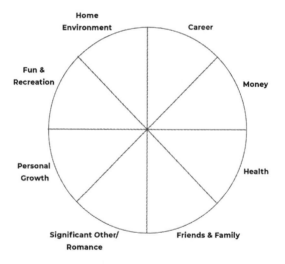

FIG 8. THE WHEEL OF LIFE.

This is Caroline's wheel of life before she started working with me. Back then, she was dissatisfied with how her career was going, feeling that she wasn't being paid her worth, which was putting her under financial pressure, and she was in a relationship that wasn't going anywhere and was full of conflict. How bumpy would the ride be if this were a real wheel?

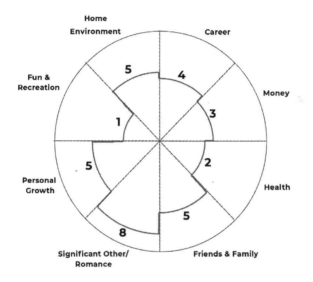

FIG 9. CAROLINE'S WHEEL OF LIFE.

By the end of the exercise, your wheel should look something like Caroline's. The new perimeter of the circle represents your wheel of life.

There are no rights or wrongs here. Your wheel is just a snapshot of how you are feeling about your life right now. It can be hugely useful to view your life in this visual way.

But what is it saying about our life? Perhaps you're getting a good salary (money 8/10) but the role you have is very stressful because of the workload and your unreasonable boss (career 4/10). You know that your health is suffering (health 5/10) and the only thing that is keeping you going is your significant other (8/10) and friends and family (7/10), but with both of those you know you are not giving them the attention they need.

How satisfied are you right now in your life? Maybe before you did this exercise you would have instinctively given yourself a 7/10, but now you've done it, you see that there are some areas that really need some attention. Which areas are they?

Ask yourself which area, if improved, would have the biggest positive impact on the others; note that this may not be the one with the lowest score. I have used this tool with hundreds if not thousands of my clients over the years, and often the area that is going to have the biggest positive impact overall is not the one they initially thought. So take your time on this.

When they ask themselves this question, many of my clients realise that if they were to focus on their own health or fun and recreation, it would positively change the other aspects of their wheel.

Well done for doing this exercise. Hopefully, it has inspired you to check in like this in the future. I tend to do this exercise at least once a quarter.

Where do you want to be?

In my experience, most people don't fulfil their potential, because they haven't spent much time thinking about what they want to achieve or where they want to go. Their New Year's resolutions have been short-term things: lose weight, do my tax return, earn more money, find a partner, visit my parents more often, hang out with my friends.

Of course, if they achieved those things, it would give them some satisfaction and a dopamine hit, but none of those achievements will really get them places.

When was the last time you spent time thinking big? Thinking about what you wanted to achieve in life? If your answer is 'not for a while', then a good place to start is by using the wheel of life you completed in the previous exercise to set yourself some goals.

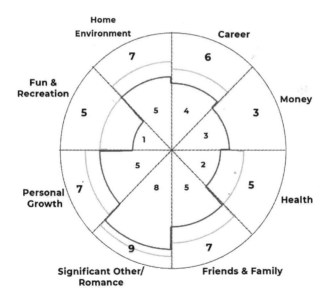

FIG 10. THE WHEEL OF LIFE.

Grab a different coloured pen and ask yourself the following question.

What time scale do I want to consider– six months, one year, two years, five years, ten years?

Choose one and then ask, 'What do I want my life to look like by then?'

Complete the wheel of life with revised lines and numbers, using a different colour from the first exercise. Don't assume you want everything to be a 9 or a 10. Think about what you really want and what is realistic in the different segments.

Now you have your desired wheel, ask yourself, 'What would need to happen for this to become reality?' For example, maybe you want to improve your career score significantly, but for that to happen you will need to focus on getting your energy back on track.

Don't assume that focusing on the biggest gap will bring the biggest results. It may be that working on something that has a small gap will give you the greatest leverage and the biggest bang for your buck.

One client I worked with had a 5/10 for her home environment, but much lower scores for significant other, friends and family, health, and fun and recreation.

But she realised that to achieve her goals and improve all her scores, she needed to move house and create an environment that really worked for her and her family. When she did the wheel of life exercise again a year later, after she had moved, all her scores had improved, even though she had not focused on the other areas directly.

What would need to happen for your goals to come about? Write down everything that comes to mind in a list in your journal. Don't censor anything. Keep the ideas coming.

Perhaps it's focusing on your career and getting promoted. Maybe it's getting your health back on track. Possibly it's changing a relationship at home or at work that you have known for some time is not working and is not good for you.

Writing these things down doesn't mean you have to take immediate action, unless of course you want to.

Keep the ideas coming and, when you feel you've written down everything you can think of, ask yourself, 'What would my older self say?' Tap into your internal wisdom and see what else comes up. You might find that now the cogs are turning; you might wake up in the middle of the night with an idea or something could pop into your mind in the shower. All good stuff. Keep the journal by your bed!

Once you have your list, start looking at it for themes, and start grouping things together. Maybe there are some goals around work or home or a relationship that fit together.

Now I want you to be ruthless. What are the *must-have* goals, rather than the nice-to-have goals? Which are the goals that would have a strong negative impact on what you want in your life if they didn't happen?

Once you have two or three of those, you can move onto the next stage. But, before we do any more, I want you to work out what's important to you.

What's driving your behaviour?

Before I had my first mental breakdown, I had no idea what was driving me. In fact, it wasn't even a question I thought of asking myself. I now know that without this awareness, I was not driving the bus. Something or even someone else was driving the bus of my life, and who knows what destination they had in mind.

If you want to be in charge of your life, be conscious of the choices you are making. To drive your own bus to your chosen destination, you need to understand what is driving your behaviour.

This area is multidimensional, with numerous possible models and philosophies. But let's keep it simple and just focus on one of the areas that drives human behaviour. Your values.

How your values play their part

Our values drive us and determine our actions. These values have often been established early on in life and are either challenged or reinforced along the way through our personal experiences.

For example, freedom might be an important value for you; in which case, as you go through your day-to-day experiences, you will be looking out for opportunities to experience freedom. It could be that you don't like being tied down to a commitment– you prefer to keep your options open. You will make decisions that increase your chances of experiencing freedom.

If you find yourself in a position where your freedom is being constrained or taken away (e.g., your employer decides to change the flexible working arrangements without consultation, meaning that you must be in the office more often), you are likely to feel huge frustration and anger.

Let's look under the bonnet and see what your values really are.

THRIVE toolkit exercise:
eliciting your values

Your values drive your behaviour. Once you understand what's going on underneath, all sorts of things will become clear, and you'll be able to make wiser choices that will honour who you are and bring you more joy.

I have found this to be one of the most life-changing exercises my clients have done, when they suddenly become aware of what's important to them, allowing them to make wiser decisions going forward.

Grab that journal again and let's get started!

Take a few moments and think about a time when you have felt life was going your way. You felt on top of the world. Things seemed easy and effortless. It could be a work-related situation, like the completion of a project. Or it could be a personal situation, when life was unfolding easily and you felt in your stride.

It doesn't matter what type of situation you choose, but choose one and write a paragraph about what was going on. What was the backdrop? Who was with you? What happened? How did it make you feel? The more information you can capture, the better.

OK, now shake it off – despite it being a lovely 'state', I need you to be able to move on to something else.

The second scenario is quite different. Now you are going to choose a time that was a real bugbear for you, a time when you were really enraged or frustrated about something. Again, it could be an episode at work or at home. You choose. Write a paragraph about what was going on, in as much detail as you can. Who was there? What was happening? How did you or others respond? The more detail the better.

Again, shake it off. You don't want to be carrying this state around for the rest of the day.

Now that you have two very different events documented, what we are going to do is identify what was going on. The chances are that in the first scenario some of your key values were being honoured, and in the second they were not. So your job now is to dig around and review what values were apparent in these scenarios.

One of my clients, called Kate, described her two situations as follows:

Scenario 1: Organising her partner's 40th birthday party

It involved: bringing Chris's closest friends together for a big bash; organising the music, food, and venue; really thinking about what Chris wanted and how she could respect his wishes; dealing with the caterers, which wasn't easy but ended up being OK once they'd had a couple of tough conversations about money and what would be provided; and dealing with the DJ and venue with ease. All in all, it was an enjoyable experience and an awesome evening. Chris loved it.

Scenario 2: Dealing with her difficult boss

Recently, Kate had found working with her boss really challenging. He didn't seem to have time for her, cancelling one-to-one meetings at short notice and not supporting her in front of others. When they did get to speak, he spent the whole time dealing with emails and even picked up calls when she was mid-sentence. He kept trying to micromanage her and give her tasks that took her away from her team and required her to work on her own. Despite Kate trying to have a conversation with him to sort things out, he wasn't interested.

The values that Kate spotted in the two scenarios were as follows:

- Autonomy

- Community

- Creativity

- Determination

- Fairness

- Friendship

- Fun

- Growth

- Influence

- Leadership

- Recognition

- Respect

- Responsibility

- Success

- Status

What values are being highlighted in your events?

Here's a list of suggestions that might help you identify what they might possibly be:

Authenticity	Curiosity	Kindness	Reputation
Achievement	Determination	Knowledge	Respect
Adventure	Doing the right thing	Leadership	Responsibility
Authority	Fairness	Learning	Security
Autonomy	Faith	Love	Self-respect
Balance	Fame	Loyalty	Service
Beauty	Friendships	Meaningful work	Spirituality
Boldness	Fun	Openness	Stability
Compassion	Growth	Optimism	Success
Challenge	Happiness	Peace	Status
Citizenship	Honesty	Pleasure	Trustworthiness
Community	Humour	Poise	Wealth
Competency	Influence	Popularity	Wisdom
Contribution	Inner harmony	Recognition	
Creativity	Justice	Religion	

Don't get hooked on these words. Choose the words that sound right to you, whether they are on the list or not.

You should have a list of five to ten words now.

Now the tougher bit. What are the top three? Identifying them might seem an impossible task, but give it a go. You might find that some of the values you have listed are similar and could be grouped, in which case do that. But come up with a list of three that feel the most important to you.

OK, great – you're nearly done.

The last part of this exercise is to ask yourself, 'Are these values being honoured in my everyday existence at work and at home right now?' Give each value a score out of 10. Add the scores up and divide by three (if you have managed to get it down to three words; if not, divide by however many words you have).

If you get an average score of seven or above, the chances are you are feeling good about life and are on your way to thriving. If, however, your average score is four or less, then you probably feel that life's not going so great. Maybe you're feeling compromised at work or home and it doesn't feel good. Don't get disheartened. It's great that you have recognised this now, because you can now do something about it!

Kate narrowed down her top three values to respect, fairness, and community. When she looked at how these values were being honoured at work and home, this is what she discovered.

	WORK	HOME
RESPECT	3	7
FAIRNESS	3	8
COMMUNITY	5	9

It was no wonder she was feeling so out of sorts at work, as her values were not being honoured. She had just been overlooked for promotion, despite having more experience than her colleague who got the job. She did not see eye to eye with her boss, who she felt did not value her contribution or behave in a respectful manner, and she was having to work on her own when her desire was to work as part of the team.

All was becoming clear, but what could she do about it? Well, unless she resigned on the spot, she knew it would take time to sort out. Armed with this new insight, she started connecting with managers she knew and liked, and looked out for opportunities that would give her a role working with others.

She was amazed how little time it took to find something and engineer her exit, moving to a place where she was going to thrive. She admitted that she would never have known what was driving her if she hadn't done this exercise and would never have found this new opportunity that she loves.

This is such a powerful exercise that can help guide you for the rest of your life. Don't miss out on this opportunity by skipping it. Do it now!

How can you play to your strengths?

*"Employees who have the opportunity to do what they do best are 57% less likely to experience burnout. Why? When people have the opportunity to **tap into their strengths**, they are more engaged, more effective, less stressed and more focused on **doing their best work** – rather than seeing their job as a burden."*

GALLUP WELLBEING REPORT 2020

According to Gallup, when you know and use your strengths, you are:

- Six times more likely to be engaged at work

- 7.8% more productive

- Three times more likely to have an excellent quality of life.

Understanding your strengths and using them in your work and everyday life is an important aspect to consider.

But how do you work out what your strengths are? Well, there are a number of ways of doing it, but one of the easiest ways I've found is to complete the online Gallup Strengths Finder. Not only does it help you identify your strengths, but it also shares how you might maximise your potential, while looking out for blind spots. Well worth the investment, I say.

Go to: **www.store.gallup.com/c/en-gb/assessments**

THRIVE toolkit exercise:
playing to your strengths

Having completed your Gallup Strengths Assessment, grab your journal and jot down your top five strengths.

- Read and understand what the assessment is telling you about your talents.

- How can you take action to maximise your potential and watch out for your blind spots?

- Ask yourself, 'How are my strengths impacting what I do, and why and how I do it?'

- How can you apply your most powerful strengths today?

- How can you ensure you minimise any potential blind spots?

- Reflecting over your career to date, notice how you felt when you were playing to your strengths... and also when you have not been able to.

How can you master your mindset?

What I mean by 'mindset' is your thoughts.

When you master your thoughts, you think differently (no shit, Sherlock!) and when you think differently, you feel differently. When you feel differently, you act differently... and when you act differently, you'll get different results.

If your thoughts and mindset are serving you right now, then carry on – but if they're not, then you have the power to change them and consequently change your life.

Sounds simple, right? Well, I agree it is simple, but that doesn't mean it's easy.

Some of your thoughts might be so habitual that you don't even realise you're thinking them. All you notice is that you feel miserable, nothing seems to be going right, and life feels like a struggle. If that is true for you, then your mindset is not serving you.

Didn't you start reading this book because you wanted things to be better? Well, if that is the case, nothing is going to change until something changes. If you continue to do what you have always done, you'll continue to get what you've always got. That's the truth of it. Nothing will change.

I believe our thoughts control our physical reality and our success much more than most people realise. Our brains are like a broadcasting and receiving station; we are sending messages all the time through our thoughts, whether we voice them or not.

Do you think that telling yourself you are stupid, fat, ugly, never going to make it, unable to cope, not smart enough or useless is helpful? What would happen if you continuously said that to another person? Do you think they would thrive, or would they wither over time, just like a child might who continues to be chastised by a critical parent?

That's right. What we say to ourselves out loud or in our heads can have a profound impact on how we feel and behave.

As Brene Brown says:

> *"Talk to yourself like you talk*
> *to someone you love."*

Nicole's story

This week I was working with a lovely client called Nicole, who was describing what a horrid time she was having with her boss. He was unfair, useless as a manager, and she hated how he undermined her confidence and showed her up in meetings.

He was a complete arse, as far as she was concerned, and she couldn't see any way out other than to leave the job she loved, in an organisation she had been in for years and felt huge loyalty to. I persuaded her to at least try a few things out before she decided to jump ship.

One of the tasks I set her was to write down all the thoughts she had before a typical meeting with her boss, who we'll call Dick.

She came up with a list that included:

- Dick will ignore me like he always does.

- He'll pick holes in everything I present and will ask awkward questions.

- The meeting will be disorganised as he's such a useless manager.

- There's going to be more conflict between us.

All these thoughts and more were getting her into a stressed state before she even arrived. She'd had a sleepless night and felt anxious, uptight and defensive. This stressed state was not serving her and was not a useful place to be.

Can you see that her state was generated by her thoughts, not by anything that was actually happening right then and right there?

Of course, she was tapping into past events and evidence... but right then, in that moment, she was creating her unresourceful state through the thoughts she was thinking.

She acknowledged that turning up to the meeting in a 'defensive grump' (her words, not mine) was not conducive to a meeting where she wanted to be heard, respected and taken seriously.

So I helped her come up with some alternative thoughts:

- I can be polite and say hello to Dick when I arrive.

- If he ignores me, there's probably something bothering him that has nothing to do with me.

- I know more about my topic than anyone else in the room.

- Whatever question they come up with, I will probably know the answer and, if not, I can find it out.

- I can help drive the content and direction of the meeting.

- I will remain calm and relaxed and allow any conflict to flow over me.

Nicole noticed that when she thought these more helpful thoughts, she felt calm, relaxed, and confident in her skin. There was a lightness and easiness about her that enabled her to be completely herself. She noticed that in this state she was her happy, smiling self.

Nicole decided to continue the experiment and try it out in her next meeting with Dick. She couldn't believe what a difference it made. She found herself enjoying the meeting and being able to influence what was going on with a confident ease. She was blown away.

Summary of SELF

In this chapter you have learnt:

Step 1: Boosting your energy

The importance of:

▶ Sleep

▶ Hydration

▶ Nutrition

▶ Moving your body

▶ Downtime

▶ Breathing properly

▶ Managing your state.

Step 2: Groundwork – who are you?

▶ Where are you now and where do you want to be?

▶ Your values – driving your behaviour

▶ Playing to your strengths

▶ Mastering your mindset

And added the following tools to your toolkit:

SURVIVE (QUICK) TOOLKIT	THRIVE TOOLKIT
STEP 1: BOOSTING YOUR ENERGY	
Sleep awareness	Nutrition review
Nutrition awareness	Changing your state
Changing your state	
Stretching your body	
Box breathing	
STEP 2: GROUNDWORK · WHO ARE YOU?	
	Wheel of life
	Eliciting your values
	Playing to your strengths

CHAPTER 5

TIME

*"Time is what we want most,
but what we use worst."*

WILLIAM PENN

What is the TIME step all about?

Understanding how you use time is a key step in the model. Are you in charge of your time, or is time in charge of you? Do you get a sense that you're in control of your day, or is it running away from you? Knowing which habits increase your productivity and focus is key. And knowing how you can buy yourself some time in this crazy fast-paced 'always on' world we are living in can make all the difference.

In this chapter I will share with you some hacks and habits that will allow you to claw back some time and be more productive so that you can achieve more and worry less.

Why is the TIME step important?

This step in the Choose to Thrive model is really important if you truly want to be productive and to thrive. You see, if you don't master this step and put yourself in charge of *your* time, you can bet your bottom dollar someone or something else will take over.

Understanding how you're using your time and deciding how you can make the biggest contribution with this limited resource is the difference between *thriving* and *striving*. And when you choose to use your time wisely, you become more productive, have greater career success and are less stressed.

What happens when you overlook TIME?

If you overlook this step, you can find yourself in all sorts of trouble. You can be overwhelmed with all the demands, choices and options.

Perhaps you get caught in the busy trap. You're up early, full of good intentions, you glance at your work phone before you jump in the shower and race off to start work where you have back-to-back meetings, with no time to think.

Then your boss unexpectedly wants to talk to you, which throws everything off. By the end of the day, you feel exhausted and disappointed. Perhaps you distract yourself with some simple tasks just to feel like you've accomplished something, but you know that all the important stuff remains undone.

You just haven't got the mental capacity at that point, and you promise you'll do things differently tomorrow. However, tomorrow never comes and you find yourself repeating the same pattern day after day.

Do not be mistaken. Busyness does not equal productivity.

Busyness ≠ productivity

It's no wonder you are feeling shattered, running from one thing to the next at a hundred miles an hour.

And not only that, you can feel wretched most of the time too; feeling on edge, out of control and guilty for not getting more done, you stay late and miss out on family and 'you time', but that just makes you feel even worse. Then Monday rolls around too soon and the whole thing starts again. It feels like you're drowning every day.

The reality is that you have to be in charge of your day, and not the other way around— even if that might feel impossible right now.

Interestingly, my recent research showed me that, regardless of the demands placed on them, some people were able to achieve more, and they did that by utilising some very specific strategies around time. And that is what I want to share with you in this chapter.

I think you're going to be very pleasantly surprised at your increased productivity and sense of thriving— that is, if you implement the suggestions. These things don't work unless you do them; it's not a spectator sport. But you know that.

Stephanie's story

Stephanie, the owner of a small business, had been working all the hours God sent for years but had not been able to make the income she wanted. She was certainly in that place of being busy but not productive. Flitting from one opportunity to the next, she was working harder and harder and longer and longer but not getting the results she wanted. She knew this was not sustainable, but she had no idea what to do about it.

I worked with her for a short period of time and focused initially on how she was using her time and her capacity to get things done. As soon as she applied the steps I describe in this chapter, things started to improve immediately.

She did a wonderful video testimonial for me, which you'll find on my website (**www.sarahsparks.co.uk**), talking about the fact that she had found the holy grail.

She now works less and earns more; in fact, she has doubled her income this year (which paid for her coaching in the first month).

Step 1: How to master time and increase your productivity

Your attitude to time

The fact of the matter is that we only have 24 hours in the day. You, me and the rest of the world. But what are we doing with these precious moments? Those 86,400 seconds every day?

We don't know how long we have on this planet; if we really thought about it, we'd realise that every second counts. But do we think of time in that way?

What happens when we find ourselves with an extra few minutes, or a spare hour or two? What do we do? Do we use that time productively and intentionally, or do we squander it?

Time is an interesting concept, because although we have 24 hours in every day, those 1,440 minutes can travel at different speeds. Have you noticed that?

When you're on a boring long-haul flight, for example, the minutes seem to last an eternity – and yet when we're with our best friends, hours pass in a flash.

In my mind, not all minutes are equal.

That being said, how could you change your thinking about time to your advantage?

I have changed my mindset towards time a lot over the years. If I find myself thinking I am short of time, I imagine the seconds ticking by really slowly and that I have more than enough time to do whatever I want or need to do. It is amazing what you can do in a short space of time.

The same is true when I want to savour something, like time with a loved one. Again, I imagine time ticking by slowly and enjoy every moment. Somehow this change of attitude towards time heightens my sense; I am more observant and have much greater enjoyment.

But the reverse is true, too. If you feel you don't have enough time, somehow the time ticks by faster. You automatically feel under pressure and that your time is running out. Not a nice feeling.

The key to changing your mindset and attitude about anything is your beliefs. Whatever you believe, your brain will seek the evidence to prove it. If you believe you are clever, you will seek evidence to prove it. And if you believe you are stupid, you will seek evidence to prove that, too.

We carry many beliefs through our entire lives without much scrutiny, and they can significantly impact the way we behave and therefore the results we get. If these beliefs are serving you, then great– but if they are not, then you have the choice to do something about it, so that they lose their grip.

Beliefs are like hungry critters that feed on evidence to keep them alive. The trick here is to feed the beliefs that serve you and starve the ones that don't.

Below are two of the most prevalent unhelpful beliefs about time.

- **I should manage my time better**: the problem with this belief is that 'time' is not the issue. Managing your priorities is the issue. It is not possible to manage time; it's a currency that will tick by regardless of what we do. But managing your priorities, choosing how to invest your time, *is* controllable by you.

- **I never have enough time**: the problem is that if you continually tell yourself you don't have enough time, you will always feel under pressure and stressed out.

By changing your mindset and telling yourself you have enough time to do the things you want to do, then you will take the pressure off, and you will start to feel on top of your to-do list. This subtle but powerful shift has an enormous impact on the way you feel about time and the things you have to do.

The next time you find yourself saying 'I don't have enough time', change the mantra to 'I have enough time to do the things I want'. It may take some practice, but you will be surprised at the impact it eventually has.

Our attitude to time determines our experience and therefore our behaviour and results. It's key to get time on your side. It's horrid to race through your days continuously feeling you don't have enough time. Read on to find out how you can achieve more, worry less and keep those stress hormones in check.

The power of a morning routine

One of my first questions when I begin coaching someone is, 'What is your morning routine?' Many of them describe waking up and forcing themselves out of bed, quickly looking at their mobile phones before jumping into the shower. Even as they brush their teeth, they may be mulling over the emails or messages they've just read and working out how on earth they are going to fit everything into their day.

They've just about left time to grab a quick breakfast— sometimes not— before they rush off to the office. When they get there, they will have just taken their jacket off when someone grabs them to ask a question. And then they're late for their first meeting, and from then they are running from one meeting to the next with no time to think.

When they get to the end of the day, they realise they are going to be late home, so they gather some overnight reading or other work, shove it into their bag and race to catch the train.

There never feels like there's enough time.

"I would be on the go from early, trying to fit in exercise before work so that I felt I was getting some balance and doing the things that mattered to me. I would be up before 5am doing a long exercise session and getting to my desk for just after 8am. During this period of my life I would start responding to emails as soon as I was awake, and when I wasn't on my email, I was thinking about it while exercising. I knew I would be in meetings throughout the day, while managing a team and their needs, and keeping on top of my emails at the same time. I tried to make myself as available as possible throughout the day, with little thought for what I might need to conserve energy. I could often be in the office until 10pm; if not, I was contactable on emails or throughout the evening."

**MID-THIRTIES WOMAN WORKING
FOR INTERNATIONAL BANK**

Even in the newer world of COVID-19, where we are working from home in 'lockdown', the same happens. People may think they have gained an extra hour or two by not having to commute, but they actually use up those hours by working longer and juggling everything around them.

It's far from a thriving way of living – but most people don't believe they have a choice or that anything could be different. That is, until they start working with me!

One of my first recommendations when I work with someone – after I've told them to get enough sleep – is to establish a morning routine. With a morning routine, you set yourself up for the day knowing what's important and requires your quality focus, and what isn't and doesn't. It grounds you in a way that stops the stress hormones kicking off so you can remain calm, clear and focused.

Personal story:
how the morning routine
changed the dragon

My nickname at Goldman Sachs was 'The Dragon' – and, on reflection, I get it. From the moment I arrived in the office, my stress levels were off the Richter scale. I was short tempered and downright rude on occasion as I was desperately trying to keep up with everything that was being asked of me and hold it all together.

From the moment I woke up at the crack of dawn (and sometimes even earlier), I was consumed by work. Checking my emails as soon as I rolled over, fretting about things in the shower, balancing paperwork I needed to read on my commute to the office (oh, those were the days), rushing everywhere, continually feeling I couldn't keep up with everything that was coming my way.

If only I had known about morning routines back then.

If you look back in history, many of the people we would consider successful had some sort of morning ritual or routine. Think of Benjamin Franklin (daily resolution), Theodore Roosevelt (reading), Oprah Winfrey (meditation), Charles Darwin (morning walk to stimulate ideas), Steve Jobs (asking, 'If today was the last day of my life, would I be happy with what I'm about to do today?'), Arianna Huffington, Barack Obama, Winston Churchill... all of them had morning routines, and the list goes on.

One of my favourite stories about morning routines is about Bianca Andreescu, the Canadian tennis player. She visualised herself winning the US Open every morning, and ended up winning it as a teenager in 2019. Powerful stuff.

So what is a good morning routine?

Over the years I have tried several different versions, but I have now landed on something that really works for me and my clients.

Ideally, I would recommend an hour for your morning routine. 'No way,' I hear you say, 'I can't do that! I don't have that sort of time!' I understand – of course you don't.

If you are a morning person, you could wake up an hour earlier to give yourself this gift. But if you genuinely don't feel you can create that sort of time in the morning, no problem. I'm also going to share a five-minute version, with the same essential points.

Once you have tried the five minutes, you may find you can build in the time to do the full hour. I do recommend taking the time to give this strategy a chance to work its magic. Then, if on occasion you need to shorten the time, you can do it with ease and still get the beneficial effects.

OK, so what to include?

THRIVE toolkit exercise:
20/20/20 vision

When I first wake up, I grab a cup of warm water with some apple cider vinegar or lemon in it and, once I've hydrated, I get started with my morning routine.

I typically do three blocks of 20 minutes first thing in the morning.

The first 20 minutes – quiet contemplation

Sit in a comfortable chair. I like to meditate, but if that's something you are unfamiliar with or struggle with (I get that when your mind is racing it's very difficult to quieten it easily), then just sit contemplating in purposeful silence. Reflect on the things you are grateful for. What you appreciate about your life. Maybe say a prayer, if that fits with you.

Be totally present in the moment. In the now. As you sit in silence, you will notice that your mind and body start to relax. If you find yourself thinking about the day ahead, don't beat yourself up; just notice it and come back to a place of gratitude and appreciation.

This may take some practice, and you might find listening to a guided meditation easier. There are plenty of approaches out there to choose from, but the ones I recommend to my clients are Calm or Headspace. You could also try Deepak Chopra's 21-day meditation challenges.

The next 20 minutes – reflecting, planning and prioritising

The world has changed so much recently that these 20 minutes are even more valuable. Ask yourself what's important now? And make it a WIN (as Greg McKeown refers to it in his brilliant book *Essentialism*). During this time, realise that you are important and need to look after yourself – because if you don't, nothing else is going to work.

What's Important Now

Because the world is changing so fast, the answer you might have given a few weeks ago might be different now. It's no good pursuing something that, even though it was right back then, is no longer relevant for now. We all need the ability to be agile and to pivot in this crazy, fast-paced world.

In reality, it's not about trying to get more things done in your day; it's about getting the *right* things done.

Ask yourself these questions:

- How am I feeling today? What's my mental form? By asking this question of yourself, you have the chance to spot when your mood starts to dip and consider what to do about it.

- What are my top inspired actions (the things that are going to give me the biggest bang for my buck) today?

- What state do I choose to be in today?

- Who are the people I need to reach out to or get in contact with today?

- How can I make a difference?

If you have some time left over, read a book or listen to a podcast. Something that inspires you or will teach you something.

The final 20 minutes – moving your body

We have already seen the importance of exercise. I find that unless I do my exercise first thing in the morning, it doesn't get done. I'm not a gym at lunch time or after work sort of girl. If you are, great. You can skip this last 20 minutes and stick to your usual routine.

If you're one of those people who has good intentions about doing exercise later in the day, which then often doesn't happen because other things take priority, I urge you to move it to the morning.

To make it easier, delegate your motivation to someone else. I don't know about you, but I'm hopeless at doing 'my own' exercise. Finding a virtual class online, where someone else is telling me what to do, is a much better idea. Change it: yoga, running, weights, dance, Pilates. Do whatever you fancy, as long as you can do it in 20 minutes.

SURVIVE toolkit exercise:
five-minute version of morning routine

I understand that for many people, the thought of carving out an extra hour each day to set yourself up for success and thriving might feel completely out of reach. So what can you do when you are short of time?

Tomorrow morning, I want you to carve out five minutes before your day starts to do the five-minute morning routine.

First minute

Sit quietly in silence. Breathe deeply and slowly, and observe your breath.

Second minute

Remind yourself of your most important priorities right now. Ask yourself, 'What's important now?'

Third minute

Sit quietly and imagine your day going perfectly. See yourself enjoying what you are doing and accomplishing what you set out to do.

Fourth minute

Get some inspiration – read one page of a book, listen to a minute of a podcast. You could also delay this part to your commute, if you have one – but if not, don't miss out on some daily learning/inspiration.

Fifth minute

Move your body. Stretch, do jumping jacks or burpees, run on the spot, put the radio on and dance... do whatever feels right that day. The idea here is to increase your heart rate so that you have more energy and are alert and focused.

Finally, pat yourself on the back and tick off the morning routine as complete on your planner. You're ready for your day.

Downtime

My God, I could write a book on this subject alone. I am beginning to think that getting some downtime is the number one challenge for folks these days.

Even my 83-year-old mother isn't willing to prioritise this part. Can you believe it?

Recently, I picked her up from the airport to drive her home. She'd flown in from Australia, so you would have thought she would be pretty tired, but the first-class travel and beds seemed to have done the trick and she was bright as a button. It wasn't until the next day, after she ran out of stories, that the jet lag kicked in.

By mid-afternoon the next day, I was tucking her up in bed and saying goodbye. Just as I was about to leave, she asked me to get her mobile phone.

'Why do you need your mobile phone, Mum, if you're off to have a sleep?'

'The phone might ring!'

I was incredulous. 'Why don't you turn it off?'

'I can't do that,' she said, and insisted on sleeping with her phone.

How crazy is that? Even my 83-year-old mother is addicted to her phone, despite spending the first 70 years of her life not having or needing one.

The world does seem to be addicted to gadgets. Everywhere you look you see people in the prayer pose, tapping into their phone or tablet, whether they are playing games, responding to messages or connecting on social media.

So what? Why does it matter?

Well, it matters because it's affecting our ability to concentrate. We are losing our focus and concentration muscle.

Our brains are wired to look for distractions because, in times gone by, distractions could mean threats or rewards. The crack of a twig indicated a predator was nearby; something moving in your peripheral vision might mean lunch was on its way.

These are all useful instincts which allowed us to survive and evolve into the advanced species we are today. But the distractions of the past were few and far between. Now they come thick and fast – and continually.

Our brains developed hundreds of thousands of years ago and haven't yet adapted to being distracted all the time. There is a part of the brain called the prefrontal cortex that is used to process information and solve complex problems. But it has a limited capacity.

Try remembering someone's phone number and doing some complicated maths at the same time. It's almost impossible unless you put down one of the items of information.

Scientists used to think that the prefrontal cortex could hold between three and seven pieces of information at any one time, but they now believe it's much fewer – maybe as little as three or four pieces at most.

That's extraordinary, isn't it? Most people are trying to juggle many more pieces of information than that at one time.

But I don't think that's the real issue. I think the real issue is that even when people are given the opportunity to focus and concentrate, they can no longer do it. They are so used to being distracted that they go and seek out distractions.

Try it! Try sitting for a while with no distractions and see how long it takes you to want to seek out something to do or touch or see or explore. We are so used to living with all our distractions that our brains get restless without them.

But again, why does that matter? Because, as Nancy Kline says, 'The quality of everything we do is dependent on the thinking we do first'.[21]

Here are some tips for getting more downtime and improving your focus and concentration.

**SURVIVE toolkit exercise:
improving your focus**

Reframe downtime as essential to productivity rather than a waste of time. Set an intention to practise downtime several times during the day. Book three sets of 10–15 minutes of downtime in your diary between meetings.

Set yourself up for success by:

• Letting others know not to interrupt you unless it's important or urgent

• Turning off notifications

• Having a 'do not disturb' symbol on your desk (one of my clients uses a pig!)

• Moving to a different location if possible. Or take a walk, or a FAB (fluid adjustment break) and stay in the bathroom!

THRIVE toolkit exercise:
planning your time

Here are some more tools for time/priority management. Using a daily and weekly planner to plan and monitor your habits can really help you stay on track.

Planning your time: daily planning

Use this daily planner as part of your morning routine. It will help you set yourself up for the day and get the most out of it.

It's a great way of helping you stay focused and nudging you to complete the healthy lifestyle choices that will retain or restore your energy and vitality.

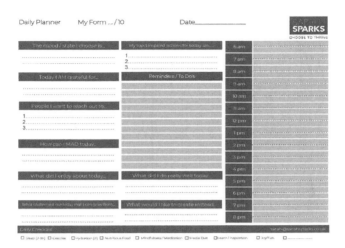

You can download a copy of this planner (and all the other planners below) from my website:

www.sarahsparks.co.uk/download-your-planner

Weekly check-in

Use this weekly check-in to consolidate the week's results and take stock.

Keeping an eye on your habits will help you to see whether you are moving towards thriving or away from it. It will help you to check if your lifestyle choices are really serving you.

There's no judgement, and no one else needs to see this. If you don't like what you see, you have the power to choose differently, and you have another week ahead to make those shifts.

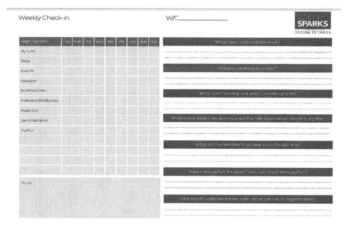

Weekly planner

Now you have taken stock of last week, what needs to be your focus this week? Use the weekly planner below to help you map out the week ahead. You'll be amazed at the difference small daily habits can make to your long-term success, progress and sense of fulfilment.

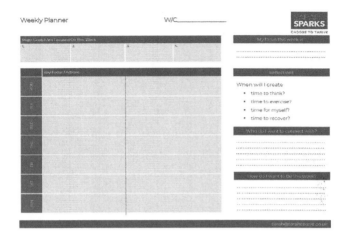

Prioritise your time

Prioritising is key. You have to choose what you are going to give your attention to. Don't let the loudest noise, or the most urgent thing, take priority without consciously being aware of what will suffer or not get the attention it deserves as a consequence.

If you don't prioritise, someone or something else will do it for you.

Have you heard of Parkinson's Law? I'll bet you've experienced it, probably quite often. Parkinson's Law is the adage that 'Work expands to fill the time available for its completion.' Have you noticed that?

Whether you have a long time before your deadline or a short time, somehow work fills the gap between now and then. Maddening!

I've certainly experienced that writing this book. I can't believe how long it's taken me. I am sure if I had set myself tougher deadlines at the beginning, I would have done it more quickly.

There are many ways to prioritise. My belief, based on working with lots of different people, is that some methods work for some people or environments and others work for other people. The key here is that you choose.

I want to share with you some different exercises that all worked for me at different times in my life. They have also worked with my clients over the years.

You see, I don't think you need to get better at time management. I think most people need to get better at priority management (or should I say self-management), which is why I want you to do the exercises that follow.

Streamline

Ever find yourself waking up in the night, wishing you had a notepad beside you (I recommend keeping one next to the bed) because you don't want to forget about something that just popped into your head?

During the day, there is so much going on in that busy brain of yours that everything gets a bit cluttered. The to-do list seems to be getting longer and longer, and there's that continuous sense of overwhelm or 'unfinished business'.

When you have fleeting glimpses of being on top of things and having a manageable to-do list, it feels so good in comparison – freeing and creative, somehow.

This next exercise will get you on your way to being in that place more often.

THRIVE toolkit exercise:
write it out

You'll need some time to do this exercise; ideally 30–60 minutes when you're not going to be interrupted. It's a great exercise to do at the weekend or when you have some time off and want to set yourself up for your return.

Grab that journal, pen, glass of water or favourite drink and find yourself a comfy chair.

First, write down all the things in your head that you think you have to do. It could be big things like 'move house' or small things like 'put out the recycling'. It doesn't matter what it is – just write it all down. No need to edit anything at this stage or try to group things. Just turn on the tap and let the thoughts flow.

I'll give you some nudges to help you keep the ideas flowing, but first just do a data dump of everything you can think of. Keep writing until you can't think of anything else.

Next, if you haven't already, write down things to do with your:

- Career (people to reach out to and network with; things you know you should do but haven't got around to yet; that thing – yes, that's the one; your expenses; all those rotas, appraisals, reports…)

- Home (kitchen, bedroom, bathroom, loft, cellar, garage, shed, shopping, recycling, rubbish)

- Family (celebrations, trips, dinners, weekends, holidays, school, doctor, dentist, shopping, admin)

- Health (doctor, dentist, physio, diet change, appointments)

- Fitness (gym, trainer, equipment, plan, challenge, accountability partner)

- Finances (sort out a pension, get an ISA, pay the bills, set up standing orders, start a savings account).

Just keep the ideas coming until you stop, then think again. When you genuinely think you have come to the end, leave a couple of pages in your journal for ideas that spring to mind later.

Now spend a moment, before you get on with the next step, just noticing what it feels like to have dumped all those things onto paper rather than having them swimming around in your head.

I remember the first time I did this exercise, on a training course at Goldman Sachs, and I could not believe the difference. I felt so much lighter for just having written everything down, rather than keeping it all in my head or on various incomplete lists. I now do this exercise regularly and it's amazing how good it still feels.

Finally, look at the list and ask yourself what has been on the list for three months, six months, nine months, more than one year?

For those items that have been on the list for over a year, ask yourself, 'Are they really important?' If they were critical, don't you think they would have been done at some point?

Now I want you to apply the three Ds to your entire list. The three Ds stand for:

- Ditch

- Delegate

- DO

Now go through the list of items and decide what can you ditch. What can you just let go of? Look for things that would be 'nice to do' but have been on the list for a while and are just not getting done. What would be the consequence of just letting them go? Would anyone apart from you notice? Do what you can to ditch as much as you can. Cross through all the items on the list that you have decided to ditch. Be ruthless.

Breathe and let them go. OK – next.

Which of the items that remain on the list could be delegated? I know you might want to do them yourself, but what is the value of having something on the list that is not being done, versus the value of getting someone else to do it (even if they don't do it perfectly or as well as you would)? How much is 'getting it done' worth to you?

Think of all the things on your list that could be delegated. Be ruthless and highlight everything. Think about:

- Who could do this task?

- What's a reasonable deadline?

- When will you delegate it to them?

And breathe. Notice how much lighter you are feeling.

"I've learned over time to let go and let my team do what they have to do, and then let them come to me when they need to. Find the right people

to work with, train them, and then give them the ability to shine or stretch in their own way."

PAT CHIN – DIRECTOR, CHIEF OF STAFF AND BUSINESS UNIT OFFICE HEAD, CITIGROUP

You should now be left with a much shorter list of items that can only be done by you. They have yet to be prioritised, but the list is a lot smaller than the one you started with.

You could go ahead and make a plan addressing how you will accomplish all of these things – but before you do, read the next section about the Pareto principle.

Use the Pareto principle

The Pareto principle, also known as the 80/20 rule, states that roughly 80% of the effects come from 20% of the causes.

Back in 1896 an Italian economist called Vilfredo Pareto showed that approximately 80% of the land in Italy was owned by 20% of the population – and an accepted fact in business management today is that 80% of sales come from 20% of clients.

If we apply this principle to clearing your to-do list, what items do you need to focus on to get the biggest bangs for your buck?

For example, it may be that by prioritising your health and wellbeing, you will be able to sustain a long and successful career, which is going to bring you the most likelihood of financial success and happiness.

Now you are thinking this way, write down the top things that need your energy and focus to give you the best results.

Create a not-to-do list

This ended up being my favourite list because it was the one that freed up the most time.

Think about how you spend a typical day at work and at home. I bet you there will be times when you are doing things that are not very useful. Spending hours on social media, for example, or watching cat videos on YouTube. What do you do that is not very productive?

If you were one of my clients, I would be asking you to keep track of a typical day and how you use your time. Many of my clients find several hours a day that are unproductive and literally time wasting.

Now, reading a magazine or gazing out of the window might be good for winding down from a stressful day. But the key thing here is to do whatever you are doing *consciously*. If you want to down tools to relax, do that. But don't just fall into checking your phone, because you won't unwind and you can't get that time back.

Believe me, I have done my share of unconsciously wasting precious time. For instance, I'm a great fan of *The Archers* on BBC Radio 4. (I know it's not everyone's cup of tea. It's a bit like Marmite; you either love it or hate it.)

If you don't know *The Archers*, it's a radio soap opera that has been going for over 70 years, about a farming family in rural England. I guess I have been listening to it for most of my life, one way or another.

The episodes run for 15 minutes at 7pm each evening and are repeated at lunchtime the following day, presumably to accommodate people's different listening patterns.

On Sundays, there's an omnibus version where you can listen to the whole week of episodes in an hour and 15 minutes. That means you could listen to the same episode three times if you put your mind to it. And that was exactly what I was doing a few years ago.

Crazy when I look back at it. Instead of investing 75 minutes into an enjoyable time listening to stories of country folk, I was investing 225 minutes every week listening to the same thing three times. That's 150 minutes wasted each week, or 130 hours every year.

What could I have been doing with those 130 hours instead? Plenty, I'd say. I now read a book, watch a TED talk or listen to an interesting podcast. Anything rather than wasting this precious life of mine.

What could you put on your not-to-do list?

SURVIVE toolkit exercise:
not-to-do list

In your journal, write down some things that need to go on your not-to-do list.

Some of my clients have put on their lists:

- Flicking through social media

- Binge-watching Netflix

- Falling asleep on the sofa

- The route to work that goes past Dunkin Donuts

- Buying biscuits or cake on the grocery order

- Working past a certain time

What could go on your not-to-do list?

Step 2: How to stay focused

Scheduling your time

Do you ever find yourself having to stay late at the office or come in early just to get your work done or create some thinking time? Maybe you use the evenings or weekends to do your work? If any of those are true for you, you probably don't schedule your time. Or perhaps you do schedule, but then something comes up and the planned time gets bumped? Am I right?

I'm going to share some recommendations I have gathered from my clients, and from research, when it comes to scheduling your time. But before I share them, let's look at why scheduling is important.

One good reason is that someone is paying you to do a job (and that includes your company, if you run your own business). Many people get distracted or pulled into tasks that are *not* their job. Maybe you have a subordinate who is under-performing and it's just easier to do their role than kick up a fuss. Possibly you've got into the habit of picking up a colleague's role to help them out, or maybe even a boss.

Whatever it is, you need to always be asking yourself – is this what I am paid for? And is it a good use of my time? If it is, carry on. If not, think about delegating (see the next chapter).

Once you have decided what is and isn't your job, the only way to get everything done efficiently, in my experience, is to schedule it as if it's an appointment with someone else. You wouldn't let them down or cancel at the last minute, right?

Ask yourself which tasks require more focus, and put those in at the times when you find it easier to concentrate. I'm a morning person, so the best time for me to concentrate is first thing, while others may focus better later in the day.

Whatever it is for you, schedule your task to match your energy and focus.

THRIVE toolkit exercise: scheduling your time

Grab your journal and your planner and look back at the exercises you did. For each item on your planner, ask yourself, 'Is this what I am being paid to do?' and 'Is this a good use of my time?'

Providing you answered yes to both those questions, you now know what's important and what you need to focus on. The question now is when to do it. Maybe you already are focusing on the important things and allocating them to your plan, which is great. But are they getting enough attention? Do they need more quality time? Without this conscious awareness and intention about how you want to spend your time, you'll find yourself torn between other people's priorities, feeling compromised as you are not making the progress you would like.

Give yourself time to think

Now you have scheduled your time to get stuff done, I suspect your diary is pretty full. Back-to-back commitments?

You're not alone with this demanding schedule. Most people fill their diaries up with back-to-back meetings but don't carve out any time to think. Then they use their own time to do the thinking work, often at the end of the day when they are exhausted.

It is a folly to miss out on quality thinking time.

**THRIVE toolkit exercise:
thinking time**

Take a look at your diary and ask yourself:

- Have I scheduled in sufficient and appropriate time to think?

- What will happen if I don't give myself enough time to think?

- What have I got coming up that requires quality thinking?

- When is the best time for me to think during a typical work day?

- How can I schedule in time to think this week, this month, this quarter?

- What will give me the biggest bang for my buck?

Jot down in your journal what you have noticed and learnt so far from this chapter.

Say no

This is something you are already good at. You're a master. You've been good at it for years. How do I know this? Because when you say yes to something, by default you are saying no to something else.

When you say yes to working late, you're saying no to going to the gym or being with loved ones. The thing is, are you conscious of what you are saying no to when you say yes to something else?

Being conscious about it makes all the difference. Otherwise, you are sleepwalking into I don't know what– and you're probably not sure, either.

Perhaps you feel that you can't say no to certain people or situations. You feel worried you might lose your job or be the first to be let go. I get it, particularly right now, but with all things there are consequences.

I know one client who sleepwalked his way into divorce. He was working so hard and for such long hours that he hardly saw his wife. She kept begging him for more time and attention, but he kept blindly going about his busyness and didn't clock the consequences until it was too late.

He thought he was doing the right thing by working hard and providing a good income for the family, but he ignored the signs and stepped over the opportunities that would have made a difference.

Knowing what you're saying no to is an important step, but it's not that easy, right? And how you say no can also be a challenge.

According to a 2013 Forbes Article called *The Art of Saying No*, research conducted at the University of California, San Francisco, showed that the more difficulty you have saying no, the more likely you are to experience stress, burnout, and even depression.[22]

Saying no is indeed a major challenge for many people, but it's also a brilliant skill to have in your pocket. When you learn to say no, you release yourself from unnecessary constraints and free up your time and energy for the important things in life.

Perhaps you can recall a time when you felt pressurised to do something that didn't feel right to you. Maybe you have found yourself saying yes when you meant no, simply because you wanted to avoid conflict.

What about times when you have felt too scared or timid to turn down a request for fear of disappointing someone? You are not alone, and I know from personal experience that these things are hard and take enormous amounts of courage.

It's not surprising that we fear saying no, because there can be consequences. We might rock the boat, stir things up or burn bridges. It might be awkward. It might damage a relationship. But the thing is, *not* saying no can cause us to miss out on something far more important: our health and wellbeing.

Saying no may cause short-term discomfort, but that's better than experiencing long-term resentment.

The thing is, when we learn how to say no gracefully, others start to respect and admire us more. They know where they stand. They start to look at us in a different light and therefore make different requests. Win/win.

The trouble with high achievers like you and me is that we often over-commit, take on too much, start to feel compromised and find ourselves under-performing.

How do you say no gracefully?

The answer is – it depends. Clearly, when you are being asked to do things against your will or your beliefs, a loud 'no' is probably going to give the clearest unambiguous message. 'No' is a complete sentence and doesn't need to be explained or justified.

But what about a 'no' in the workplace? Below are some suggestions for how you might come up with a graceful 'No' at work:

- I'm flattered but I don't have the bandwidth right now.

- I would have liked to, but I am over-committed.

- I'd be happy to help on this, but I can't look at it until the end of the month.

- I'm sorry I can't help you with that, but I know someone who can.

- Let me check my calendar and I'll come back to you.

- Yes, happy to do this, but what would you like me to de-prioritise?

- You're welcome to... and I will...

That last one is great with kids. Yes, you're welcome to make yourself a snack, and I will leave you to tidy up afterwards. Here you are making clear what the deal is.

You'll find using humour is also a great way of saying a graceful no. Saying 'no' is a true leadership capability and is not seen often enough, in my view. But it takes practice as well as courage.

I can highly recommend honing this skill. It enables you to be in charge of your time and in charge of your life.

The thing is, what you don't do is just as important as what you do.

You can do anything, but you can't do everything.

THRIVE toolkit exercise:
saying 'no'

Write in your journal: 'Right now, I am saying no to…'

List all the things that you are saying 'no' to because of your commitments to work. For example:

- Exercising
- Socialising with friends or family
- Finding a partner
- Looking after your health and wellbeing
- Getting enough sleep
- Meditating
- Having some downtime
- Doing hobbies
- Spending time with the kids

Jot down all the things that are important to you that you are saying no to because you are saying yes to something else. Focusing on what you're giving up makes it easier to say no.

Next, consider who you need to say no to right now. Is it a particular boss or team or colleague? Jot their names down.

Now you have identified the key people, think about separating the request from the person. If someone else was making the same request, would it be easier to say no? Would you negotiate differently?

For example, maybe the CEO is keen to have a particular report on their desk by the end of the week, but it will be a struggle to complete it unless you give up some of your personal time. What if the same request was being made by a colleague rather than the CEO? What would you do then?

Think about the key things you want to say no to right now and consider how you might say it gracefully. Choose some of the less high-stakes items and have a go. Remember, when you decide to say no, avoid phrases such as 'I don't think I can' or 'I'm not certain'.

Come back and write down what you have learnt and how you feel. What could you do differently next time that would make it easier for you and still get you the results you want?

Saying no to a new commitment means you can success-fully fulfil your existing ones. When you learn to say no, you free up your time and energy for the important things in your life.

Focus your concentration

How are your levels of concentration? Are you finding it more difficult to focus than you used to? It's not really sur-prising; not only is the world full of distractions, but we have also lost the ability to concentrate.

I believe that focused concentration is a bit like a muscle: either you use it or you lose it. Most people are giving in to distractions and losing their concentration muscle.

I would even go a step further. I believe people who can focus and concentrate will be the success stories of the future, and they will be quite a rare breed.

I spoke earlier about the brain hormones and how never in the history of mankind have there been so many distrac-tions and demands on our attention. You know what it's like: you sit down to do something and all sorts of other things demand your attention.

Finishing off a small task, emailing your boss about some-thing you've forgotten to share with them, responding to a message that has just appeared, adding something to your diary or your shopping list, or thinking about what's for supper can all distract you from the task in hand. There are all sorts of ways of being distracted.

If you've been working from home, your housemates can also be a distraction, whatever their ages.

It takes quite an effort to set up your environment and commit to doing some focused, concentrated work. Why bother? You're good at multitasking, right? *Wrong!* Even if you are good at switching between tasks, it's a massive drain on your energy and ability to get things done. Don't do it.

As we saw earlier, there is no such thing as multitasking: performing multiple tasks at once is a process that requires your brain to disengage and re-engage constantly. It's draining and inefficient. Not only that: it changes our brain wiring and therefore our behaviour, resulting in less empathy and emotional control.

Instead of multitasking, you need to build your concentration muscle by retraining your brain to stay focused.

"The thing that I think was critical for me, was this feeling of always being reachable. Even when I was in the office, if I was in a meeting, I would be on my phone or on my iPad responding to emails. Someone would be contacting me about something urgent, so I'd have to step out of the meeting. Or if I was at my desk on a conference

call, a member of my team would come up and talk to me. It felt like there was always this bubble around me of people contacting me, either by email, by messenger, or speaking to me when I was meant to be focused on another task.
That is just exhausting, because your brain is split the whole time."

MID-THIRTIES WOMAN WORKING FOR INTERNATIONAL BANK

"I had a textbook high-performing career, I suppose, from the moment I qualified. And I made partner quite early. And I had, certainly in my first year of partnership, a number of extremely large, valuable mandates – by which I'm talking about multi-billion-pound deals – which is where some of the catastrophising came in. I was really, really busy in my first couple of years. And I suppose I got to a stage where I was constantly exhausted, couldn't really keep any perspective on the magnitude of what I was doing, crying at my desk over nothing, and I just thought all of that was normal. I just thought that's the kind of stress that a brand new junior partner goes through. My first year of partnership was the hardest year of my life. When I was sitting reading these big documents, and I'd be *reading for an hour, and I'd turn two pages, and I had no idea what I'd read. And that then started a spiral of catastrophising because I'd be thinking, oh my God, I'm signing off on these transactions, and I've got no idea what's on the documents. I am just a negligence case waiting to happen and constantly feeling on the edge of my seat because I didn't know what was happening in these documents."*

SAM BROWN – PARTNER AND HEAD OF PENSIONS AT HERBERT SMITH FREEHILLS

THRIVE toolkit exercise:
focus

Before we start: you will need your journal and 20 minutes of uninterrupted time.

Sit down and choose a topic you love. It could be cats, gardening, music, sport. It doesn't matter what it is – just choose a topic.

Write anything and everything about your topic. It doesn't need to make a lot of sense; just try and keep writing.

While you are writing, notice what else happens. Mark in the margin every time your brain goes off-piste and onto another topic or task. See how many other unrelated thoughts pop into your mind. Your holiday plans, birthday celebrations, what you want to do this weekend, and all the rest.

Unless you regularly meditate or do 'deep work', you'll be surprised just how busy your brain is and how difficult it is to make it concentrate for any length of time.

Don't panic. You are not alone. Most people are suffering the same thing.

But that's where the opportunity lies. When you can retrain your brain to focus and concentrate for periods of time, you will be in the minority, and you will be able to chomp through work like there's no tomorrow.

I believe this is a skill that is worth cultivating, but the bottom line is that no one else can do this for you. It's like touch typing – you must put in the hours of practice, but it's absolutely worth it when you do.

Get priming

But that's not all you need to do. The next thing is called priming. What do I mean by that? Well, priming is getting yourself and others ready. This is particularly important for the deep concentration work.

Have you ever experienced this? You've scheduled time into your diary to do a particular task, but find yourself thinking 'Oh, I'd better just send that email first' or 'I'll just pop to the loo'. And then it's 'Oh I need a glass of water or a coffee'... and by the time you sit down again, you have already lost 10 or 15 minutes.

And then as you finally begin work, an email or text comes in and you just can't resist looking at it, or someone is hovering outside your door and not going away. Have you ever found that?

This is why priming is so important. For tasks that require deep levels of concentration and focus – the ones where your organisation is wanting to use your intellect most effectively – you need to get yourself and those around you ready so you can concentrate and have uninterrupted focus time.

This a dying art, and it's dying swiftly. Most people have lost their ability to concentrate and do focused work because they are so used to being interrupted.

But why is it important? Research shows that if you are deep in concentration and get interrupted, it takes 23 minutes to get back to that same level of concentration.[23] Yes, you read that right: 23 minutes! That is extraordinary, isn't it?

The reality is that if you want to do deep quality work that requires concentration, you not only need to carve out the time to do it, but you need to set up that time to be uninterrupted and start training your brain to focus for longer periods.

How can you get yourself and others primed and ready to go?

Prime yourself

Let's start with you. What are the things you need to consider?

I tend to check in with my physiology first and make sure I have any FAB (fluid adjustment break) I need for the task ahead. I also make sure I have sufficient sustenance. If I am even remotely hungry, I know I will find that a distraction and I also know it will impact my brain capacity, so I need to eat.

I make sure there is a healthy snack to hand in case I have an energy dip – a banana or some nuts, for example.

Then I get all my gadgets ready. I turn off mobile phones, laptop notifications, even my landline; anything that could go buzz or ping. I have even been known to leave notes for the postman to leave the delivery outside rather than knock on the door. Whatever it takes to be fully present and be able to focus on the work at hand.

Prime others

Just as I am writing this, my housemate interrupts my train of thought to say goodbye. How ironic! You see, although

I have agreed with him that the first two hours of my working day are dedicated to writing this book until it's complete, we hadn't agreed about interruptions – or clearly not well enough, anyway.

If he had thought about it, he could have seen that I was in the middle of writing something. But no, he was in his world and came in without thinking. Seems a small thing, doesn't it? But interruptions like this really can affect your productivity and concentration. Remember those 23 minutes?

So back to priming others. The key here is that agreements avoid disagreements! Let the people around you know. Tell them why you're doing what you're doing and why it's important for you to be able to get this done. Agree between you under what circumstances it would be OK to interrupt you, because there are bound to be some. Maybe there is a certain client you need to prioritise that day, or a call from a loved one that you'd like to make an exception for. But even then, it's better to forward your phone so that someone else answers it and can ask the caller if they could call you back at a certain time.

Get your team around you to support you by intercepting anyone who looks like they may interrupt your flow; you could do the same for them when they need it.

If you work in an open-plan office, or at home, have an agreed signal on your desk that symbolises to others that this is your focus time. One of my clients has a fat pink pig that is put on her desk when she wants to focus. Another wears his headphones as his way of communicating to the world 'don't interrupt me'! Interestingly, he doesn't even listen to anything. It's just his way of having greater peace and quiet and blocking out the surrounding noise.

Whatever you need to do, set yourself up to focus and concentrate – as they (almost) say in the Nike ad – JFDI!

Take a break

Of all the recommendations in this book, this next one is high on the priority pile. It takes courage, consistency and downright determination to do this – but if you don't, the chances are that you are just not functioning at your best.

Think about it. If you were a hardened smoker, you would regularly go and take cigarette breaks. You wouldn't feel guilty about it. You would say to someone, 'just off for a ciggy', or something similar. You'd then take a walk out-side, find a quiet corner, light up and take a long drag. You might stay there for 10–15 minutes, pondering your day, before heading back.

What if everyone gave themselves permission to step out of their busy day for a short period of time? My belief is that productivity would increase, as well as mental well-being.

Let's look at the benefits of this short break:

- You can get some perspective by stepping away from what you are doing.

- You physically move and get the blood and oxygen circulating.

- You get some daylight (away from the damaging blue screens).

- You get a moment to breathe deeply, filling your lungs, body and brain with oxygen.

- It allows you time to make meaning of what you are working on.

- It increases the likelihood of a Eureka moment by making new connections/meaning.

This ritual is undoubtedly good for you and your focus, concentration, productivity and wellbeing. But how many of the non-smokers allow themselves these breaks during the working day? Very few, I would wager.

Ask yourself 'why?'

I am sure part of it is lack of awareness but, even when people do know the benefits, they struggle to actually take breaks. Often organisational culture and expectations don't encourage such behaviour. Maybe they have a boss who believes that to be productive you need to be seen to be working, or possibly they – or you – have linked taking breaks to laziness.

The same is even true for lunch breaks; many people feel they cannot step away from their desks to take a lunch break for fear of what their bosses will think of them. So they keep on ploughing through their to-do lists, slowly but surely becoming less productive without even knowing it.

I know in the past I didn't give myself permission to take a break, even though everything inside my body was screaming for a moment of rest. My brain didn't work, I couldn't think straight and yet I just felt I needed to keep going. It was nonsense looking back, but that is easy to say now. At the time, it was how I really felt: I just didn't think I could afford a break and certainly didn't understand the reasons behind why I should.

Have courage

Let's use sport and going to the gym as the metaphor. Perhaps you know what it's like if you overdo it in the gym? You've been away from the gym for a while and you want to get back into it, so you go back and start lifting the weights and doing the circuits you were able to do when you left off.

And probably the next day you're barely able to walk. Going up and down stairs is agony. You've well and truly overdone it, and now you're going to have to wait a few days before you can start again – how daft was that?

In sports terms, you've over-trained. You pushed your muscles way beyond what they were capable of, caused some damage and now you need to give yourself some time to recover.

Sports people the world over know the dangers of over-training; serious athletes avoid it at all costs. Instead, they focus on giving their body just-manageable challenges then – crucially – allowing themselves time to recover.

We don't do that in the business world. But if you continue to push yourself, like I did, for years then finally your body and brain say 'enough' and shut down. That is what it literally felt like for me. My brain just shut down. That strategy cost me big time, and I don't recommend it.

**SURVIVE toolkit exercise:
commit to a lunch break**

First, as part of your morning routine, grab your planner and decide when you intend to stop for lunch. Schedule it in and decide what will be the nudge for you to say, 'Lunch time – time to stop.'

If you don't feel you can take an hour, that's OK – but as a minimum, plan at least 20 minutes to step away from your desk and re-nourish your body with nutritious food, hydration, movement and fresh air.

Second– again, as part of your morning routine– look at your commitments today and decide when would be good to take a fluid adjustment break. Mark it in the planner. I am not suggesting this is the only time you can step away and take a bathroom or tea break – far from it – but at least take a break at some point in the morning and afternoon to keep your energy and productivity high.

Step 3: How to buy yourself more time

Hack back your emails

Emails are the bane of many corporate executives' lives. I have had clients who couldn't possibly even read, let alone action, all the emails they got, even if they spent all day doing so– and, of course, they had other things to do too. It's crazy just how many emails some executives get.

Clearly, that's not useful or sustainable. Often these execs are being paid a lot of money to get things done. The fact that they are having to trawl through hundreds of emails to find the ones that really matter is hugely time consuming and costly.

There are lots of recommendations and books written solely about managing emails, which you can access if you want to. What I'd like to do here is to share some basic principles that I hope will help if you are currently being overrun.

These principles are to reduce the number of emails, create a specific time to read and action them, and shorten the time taken to respond. Let's take those one by one.

Reduce the number of emails you get

Be ruthless with your inbox. Unsubscribe from anything that is not serving you.

There are useful apps to help you do that, like cleanfox. io and clean.email – the former is free but states it sells its anonymous data, while the latter costs £8 a month. Be careful about the terms and conditions of free services, as they will all be making money somewhere.

Another way to reduce the number of emails you receive is to send fewer emails.

Really think about it before you send the next email. Is it adding value or just filling up the ether? Does it need to go to so many people? How can you reduce the chances of getting an email response back?

I am not suggesting here that you stop sending important emails to key people– just ask yourself if it's absolutely necessary. If the answer is yes, go ahead. If not, don't send it, and feel proud that you are not stealing others' time.

Look at all the emails you are being copied in on. Is it necessary for you to be on each of these cc lists? Maybe something is interesting to know but not vital for your job and not what you're paid to be on top of. Perhaps you could ask to be notified if something specific happens and politely ask to be removed from the 'to all' distribution, citing email overwhelm, if necessary.

Another way to reduce the number of emails you receive daily is to delay delivery of your emails. Chances are that some of the issues may have been addressed by the time you had intended to send your response, so in which case 'job done' – the email is no longer necessary.

Create a boundary time to read (and action) emails

To be productive, you must be able to focus, so it's no good distracting yourself every few minutes to read emails and potentially respond to them. It's much better to decide up front when you are going to look and respond to emails so that you can be in charge of your day, rather than the other way around. Don't allow your inbox to be the boss.

Carve out a specific time and duration for emails. It could be between 9 and 10am, for example. Scan the subject headers for topics that relate to your top priorities; look at those messages and respond to them first.

Now scan the remaining emails and, without looking at the messages themselves, delete anything you already know will not be a good use of your precious time.

Then decide on the next most important emails to respond to. Be really clear on the boundary of how long you've got. Get your head down and get through as many as you can.

If there are emails remaining at the end, you need to decide what to do with them. Can they be delegated? What if you just didn't respond? What would happen then?

If you can't address all the emails in the allotted time, but you want to, you'll need to carve out additional time at another point in the day. Don't allow the boundary to be leaky– don't just keep doing emails to get them out of your inbox. Have the courage to step away.

Technology itself can help you manage the tsunami of emails. You can now preprogram when you receive and can send emails. This is a great evolution; many people don't have the same level of discipline that you are now creating, and sending and receiving emails out of your normal office hours can have a detrimental effect on your own and others' rest and recovery time and mental health.

Think to yourself, 'Am I adding to others' pressure? Does this email really need to be sent now or can it wait until later?'

Shorten the time taken to respond to emails

Pareto's law can really have a field day when it comes to responding to emails. Many people spend hours composing a reply when a short, succinct response (or even just picking up the phone) would be just as effective. Instead of taking time to think and craft every word, a quick response or discussion can often be enough to move things to the next stage, or even resolve them.

Of course, some emails need a thorough and in-depth response, but others really don't. Before you start writing chapter and verse, ask yourself, 'What is the essence I want to say here? What is the most succinct way I can say it?' However, I do realise this doesn't suit everybody's personality.

Some people use long emails to show off their knowledge and experience, but seriously, do *you* really need to do that?

Keep your emails short and clear wherever possible, knowing you are clawing back precious time as well as gifting extra time to the recipient.

Ditch unnecessary meetings

Whether you are working from home or back in the office, if you have a schedule full of meetings the chances are that at least one or two in the week are not really adding to where you need to focus your time.

Perhaps some of these meetings are essential, but maybe not. Perhaps these meetings have been going on for years, and attending them is a bit of a habit.

As with emails, the best thing to do with meetings is to be ruthless. Ask yourself:

- Do I really need to attend?

- Could someone else go in my place?

- Could someone else update me on the key points in less time?

- Am I really adding value by attending this meeting?

- Is it what I am being paid to do?

**SURVIVE toolkit exercise:
meetings**

- Take a look at your meetings for the next week.

- Which ones are 'must attends'? And why?

- For the remaining meetings, who could go on your behalf?

- Which meetings should you decline? (Refer to the 'graceful no' techniques.)

Just imagine how it will feel when you can release some of your precious time to do the things you want to do. Be brave and courageous, dear reader. It will pay dividends.

Summary of TIME

Mastering your relationship to time is vital if you want to be successful, feel on top of things and thrive. There is no getting around it. As I mentioned earlier, it's not really a time management issue. It's a mindset and self-management issue.

Only you can choose what is the best use of your time and where you should focus this precious and limited resource.

In this chapter you have learnt:

Step 1: Increasing productivity

The importance of:

▶ Attitude and mindset

▶ A morning routine

▶ Tools for priority management

▶ Prioritising your time.

Step 2: Staying focused

The importance of:

▶ Scheduling your time

▶ Creating time to think

▶ Saying no

▶ Focused concentration

▶ Taking a break.

Step 3: Buying yourself more time

The importance of:

▶ Hacking back your emails

▶ Setting boundaries for email time

▶ Shortening your email responses

▶ Ditching unnecessary meetings.

And you have added the following tools to your toolkit:

SURVIVE (QUICK) TOOLKIT	THRIVE TOOLKIT
STEP 1: INCREASING PRODUCTIVITY	
Five-minute morning routine	20/20/20 vision
Improving your focus	Write it out
Not-to-do list	Planners
STEP 2: STAYING FOCUSED	
Commit to a lunch break	Scheduling your time
	Thinking time
	Saying no
	Focus
STEP 3: BUYING YOURSELF MORE TIME	
Ditching meetings	

CHAPTER 6

OTHERS

"The single biggest problem with communication is the illusion that it has taken place."

GEORGE BERNARD SHAW

What is the OTHERS step all about?

Understanding how to get the best out of others is key to success. It always has been and I suspect that, despite the world changing rapidly around us, it always will be. We really can't be successful in isolation.

But there is another aspect of our relationship to others that is important too, and that is having a mindset of service and contribution. Why does that matter? Well, when you have a mindset focused on how you can serve and contribute to others, it feels good, you want to do more of it, and you will overcome challenges differently.

You can't be a good leader without a following, and that comes down to your communication and its effectiveness. But if you want to be a great leader, you'll want to know that what you are doing is making a difference.

In this chapter I will share some key strategies and skills for communication and contribution that, once mastered, will take the stress out of interacting with others and lead to greater impact, greater confidence, and greater success.

Why is the OTHERS step important?

If you think about all the most stressful episodes in your life, I'd bet my bottom dollar that all of them included someone else. Perhaps they involved a heated exchange with a colleague, a misunderstanding with a boss or friend, a subordinate that just didn't seem to be getting it.

Even if you have mastered your SELF and TIME, it won't be long before you find yourself struggling– until you have mastered this next step: OTHERS.

I don't mean that in the derogatory sense of controlling or manipulating others; quite the contrary. Most people in this connected world really can't thrive or even function without interacting with others. We are social animals, after all.

What happens when you overlook OTHERS?

If you overlook this step, your life will be full of challenging episodes. You might feel disappointed or frustrated at your interactions with others. And you might even get a reputation for being difficult and troublesome, so that people avoid dealing with you and you become more isolated and out of the loop. When this happens, interactions with others feel awkward, things take longer to do, and life's just hard work.

In addition, if you have no sense of service and contribution you might find that work is like wading through treacle and just not enjoyable.

Client story:
Charlotte, a long-overlooked employee

I met Charlotte in the bowels of a bank a few years ago. She was tearful, despondent, overwhelmed and defeated. She'd been with an international bank for 18 years and had progressed along the way, but recently had been turned down three times for promotion.

She had great reviews, received excellent feedback from her team and achieved all her KPIs, but somehow that wasn't enough. As far as she was concerned, she felt she had met the female glass ceiling and nothing was going to change the pale, male, stale leadership around her.

She was even told, 'You're not as good as you think you are.' Highly motivational – not! Her boss just didn't seem to understand her, and she didn't like him.

As I worked with her, she soon realised she could not allow this situation to get her down, or to continue. She needed to do something about it, but she didn't know where to start.

I shared with her some key strategies that I am going to share with you, and I helped her see how, by changing her own behaviour, she could improve her ability to impact and influence.

By improving her relationships with key stakeholders – her boss in particular – she would have a different experience at work. She went back into the workplace with a new spring in her step. She had nothing to lose and everything to gain. And it worked.

People began to notice the shift in her and started to pay more attention to what she was saying. The more they noticed, the more she thrived and shared her brilliance. Even her boss started to notice things were different. Of course, she didn't get promoted overnight, but she kept up her confidence and her strategy... and I remember to this day the call I got, when she rang with such excitement in her voice to say thank you and that she'd been promoted.

Whether we are talking about communication or contribution, the bottom line is that we're talking about interacting with others, which means your journal work will be different in this section.

I hope you've noticed and enjoyed that the exercises I have set you so far have been experiential. I believe that true learning only happens at an experiential level and can't be experienced theoretically in the same way.

But in this section, you are not going to be able to do these exercises in isolation. You are going to have to get out there and try new things. Remember Henry Ford's sage advice: 'If you keep on doing what you've always done, you'll keep on getting what you've always got.'

If you really want to change your results in this area, you are going to have to interact with people differently; you can't just make some notes in your journal. It may take courage, but it will be worth it, and you will be surprised at the effect changing the way you interact with others will have on you and your success.

First, let's look at the different aspects of communication that I believe will make all the difference and I wish I had been taught when I was much younger. It would have made such a difference, saved many sibling arguments, probably enabled me to stay married, and would certainly have made my career more successful and less stressful.

OK, here goes.

Step 1: Communicating with others

> *"I've learned that people will forget what you said, people will forget what you did, but people will never forget how you made them feel."*

MAYA ANGELOU

Most people have no idea what they are communicating to others.

Think about it: you can tell what sort of mood someone is in when they walk into the room, right? It's obvious whether they are in a foul mood and need to be given a wide berth or in a good mood and it's going to be fun to hang around with them.

We communicate all the time without speaking. And, if we don't consider how we are coming across, we will run into trouble.

Have you come across the 7/28/55 rule? This piece of research is often misquoted; however, I think it is still interesting to consider.

In 1968 Dr Albert Mehrabian published his research into communication of feelings and attitudes.[24] He concluded that the words, tonality, and body language have different relative influences: words 7%, tonality 28%, and body language 55%.

Furthermore, he discovered that if there was any incongruence between these different channels of communication, the person receiving the message would become irritated and confused.

Discovering that the words we say are nowhere near as important as the way we say them (our tonality and body language) is a massive wake-up call to many.

You may have experienced this at first hand when someone says something but you 'don't believe a word of it'. It could be a friend who is feeling miserable but replies 'I'm fine' to the question 'How are you?'

So what are you communicating? In your last meeting, what were you communicating non-verbally? Were you communicating a 'good' or 'bad' mood? Were you communicating 'I'm stressed', 'There isn't enough time', or 'I'm feeling out of my depth'? Were your words aligned with how you felt, or were you sending mixed messages? All interesting stuff, and useful to start thinking about.

It's time to be more aware and intentional about how you come across. It will serve you well. So what are the different aspects of communication you really need to master?

Seek first to understand

If you're like most people, the chances are that in your interactions with others you're keen to get your point of view across. You're excited and you jump in with ideas and solutions that make obvious sense to you. That's what you're being paid for, right?

You pretend you're listening but sometimes your attention wanders; you pick up on certain parts of the conversation, but maybe miss the meaning entirely. Why does this happen?

It's because most people listen with the intention of replying and not with the intention of understanding. You listen to the other person while preparing in your mind what you are going to say next. Everything you hear is filtered through your frame of reference – your beliefs and your experiences – and you decide the meaning before the other person has finished speaking. Do you think you've ever done that?

Learning to communicate effectively is one of the most important life skills. Even if you believe this is already one of your skills, there is always something you can learn.

Client story:
Simon, learning to listen

Take Simon, a successful executive, who turned up at one of his coaching sessions venting about how useless his new manager was. He felt that his new boss was a bad manager, making 'crap decisions' and sending the team in the wrong direction.

Simon didn't like what I said next, but it was said with a good positive intention, and he later agreed that it changed his life. I asked him, 'Have you spent time with your new boss to understand all the facts? Have you listened to and heard your boss, so you really understand what's behind his thinking?'

Although Simon was convinced he already knew all the facts, he decided to sit down for a coffee with his boss and have an open and honest conversation about why he'd made his recent decisions.

As they talked, it became clear that Simon only had half of the story. Once he had heard the full 360-degree view of why his boss had made the decisions he had, and saw their actual outcomes and impact on the team, he realised he'd jumped to conclusions and made assumptions... and you know what they say about assuming!

If you really want to make an impact on others, your first port of call is to seek to understand first before trying to be understood– even if you're someone's boss and you don't think you should have to.

If your subordinate is not doing what you want them to, then first and foremost you have an understanding problem. Sit down and have a conversation to under-stand what is really going on before you decide your next course of action. You will reap rewards aplenty.

THRIVE toolkit exercise:
understanding your relationships

Here's the rub. As I mentioned at the start of this section, we're now talking about *others* so, while I have included some journal work, you're going to have to get out there and experiment if you want to make change in this area.

Grab your journal and:

- Write a list of people you would like a better relationship with. It could be a sibling, boss, colleague, partner, child. Write down everyone who comes to mind.

- Rate those relationships out of 10, where 10 is an awesome relationship in which you both feel understood and 1 is a relationship fraught with stress, misunderstanding and even possibly disdain.

- In a separate column, rate out of 10 how important that relationship is to you, where 10 is very important and 1 is not very important.

- Looking at your list, highlight the top three relationships that have a low relationship score but a high importance score. For example, Helen, Fiona and Mike in the table below.

	RELATIONSHIP	IMPORTANCE
SAM	5/10	9/10
NEVILLE	7/10	2/10
PETER	2/10	2/10
FIONA	3/10	9/10
MIKE	4/10	10/10
DOUG	5/10	5/10
HELEN	2/10	9/10

You now have your top target relationships.

- Take a moment and ask yourself what it will be like when these relationships are on a more even footing and have a higher relationship score. How will you feel? What difference will it make? Write down a couple of points for each relationship.

- Now think about the next interactions you have coming up with these key people. It might be on Zoom, or face to face, or even via email.

- Plan to 'first seek to understand before I am understood'. Allow that thought to really sink in, and have it in the forefront of your mind just before you start interacting with the other person.

- As you keep in mind this intention – I will first seek to understand before I am understood – notice how you interact differently. Notice, too, how the other person responds. As with all things, these skills take practice, so just give it a go. Don't expect miracles overnight, but do notice when things start to change between you.

- Continue your interactions in this manner, and at the end of the week score the relationships out of 10 and see what's different now.

- Write a couple of comments against each relationship, reminding yourself of the things that really worked and that you plan to do again.

For relationships that have been on the rocks for some time, even this small, subtle shift can have a profound impact. But that's not all. Read on…

The impact of listening

> *"You cannot truly listen to anyone and do anything else at the same time."*

M SCOTT PECK

Listening needs a section of its own. It's a skill that most people would probably say they are pretty good at. But if you did the previous exercise, perhaps you will already have done more listening in the exercise than you would usually do.

Some people might argue that they listen by default. Unless you are actually deaf, then you must be listening, right?

WRONG!

There is hearing and then there is *listening*. Of course, our brains are scanning for danger all the time and our ears play a key part in that, so at some level we are always 'listening'.

But are we consciously listening, or are we just hearing sounds? Listening involves understanding. It also involves judgement and filtering. In any conversation that has involved praise and criticism, how much focus have you put on the positives and how much on what could be improved?

There are different levels of listening; we adopt each one depending on the situation, and they overlap and interchange. Let's call the deepest level of listening – where you have the highest potential for understanding and retention – level 1, or active listening. At the opposite end, there's level 3, where you physically take in the sounds but you block out the meaning.

Most people would find it difficult to stay in level 1 listening during a highly conflicted situation, when they are being threatened, or when they feel anxious or angry. This is all normal and happens outside of your awareness. Others listen very effectively when they are working, only to tune out when they arrive home. Have you ever done that, or do you know someone who does?

Level 1

If you want to influence, you have to be able to listen effectively and understand. That means training your brain to listen at level 1 when it matters.

But how do you make sure you are engaged in active listening?

When someone else is talking, an active listener gives their full attention to what is being said. They already know that listening properly will give them new and useful information, so they don't allow themselves to be distracted.

They remain fully engaged and alert throughout the interaction, paying attention to all aspects of the communication: the words, the tonality and the body language. They encourage the speaker to share by nodding encouragement and keeping eye contact.

They check their understanding; they know that words mean different things to different people, and so they paraphrase the message back to the speaker to give an opportunity for clarification.

They use empathy to step into the place of the speaker and try to see things from their point of view. They are aware of their own biases and attitudes, and suspend their own thoughts and feelings.

Level 1 listening is a full-on experience for both the speaker and the listener.

Level 2

The next level of listening is level 2, otherwise known as passive listening. The passive listener hears the words but does not really listen. This can lead to all sorts of misunderstandings and possible conflicts.

Unlike level 3, where it is obvious the listener is not listening, level 2 listening can give the false impression that the speaker is being listened to and understood.

However, someone listening at this level does not attempt to understand the deeper meaning of what the speaker is really trying to say, and instead stays on the surface. They listen logically and are more concerned with the content of the message than the feeling behind it.

They remain emotionally detached from the conversation. They assume it is the responsibility of the speaker to ensure the success of the communication.

Level 3

Level 3 is called non-listening. In this situation, it's pretty clear that the listener is tuning in and out.

They are mainly paying attention to themselves and their own thoughts. They pay just enough attention to what's being said to give them a chance to talk. They listen quietly and unresponsively. They may fake attention while they are thinking about unrelated matters or preparing what to say next.

Just imagine you're giving a pitch to a potential new client.

- **In scenario 1** they are nodding along and asking you to clarify points. You get the sense they are really interested in doing business with you.

- **In scenario 2** they nod occasionally, but they're not asking many questions. You get the sense they have other things on their mind, but feel they need to be polite.

- **In scenario 3** you can tell they are not interested. In fact, they are making that pretty clear by burying themselves in their phone and avoiding any eye contact. The only time they speak is to say, 'Are we done?'

Which of these pitches do you think would be successful?

Very few people spend most of their time listening at level 1. You have probably found yourself in a meeting thinking about what you need to buy at the supermarket (level 3). Maybe you have been so incensed with what someone has just said that you are thinking about how you are going to respond (level 2).

Most of us listen at all three levels over the course of a day, but the more we listen at level 1, the more effective we will be as leaders.

THRIVE toolkit exercise:
active listening

Think about the last meeting you had. What level of listening were you in most of the time? What difference would it have made if you had spent more time in level 1 – active listening?

What meetings have you got coming up where you want to make a good impression and/or be able to influence someone?

As you think about these meetings and the likely participants, what level of listening do you want to demonstrate?

How might you do that? Take another look at the active listening behaviours and think about how you will demonstrate these in this meeting.

After the meeting, jot down what was different when you deliberately listened at level 1.

Notice, too, situations in which you habitually listen at level 2 or 3. What are the consequences? What would you like to change in your next interactions?

What happens when you have a different opinion to the other person? What level of listening are you doing then?

Are you at level 1 or are you just composing what you are going to say next?

The next time you have a different point of view, why not put your curious hat on, while focusing intently on what the other person is saying, and ask yourself, 'What am I missing?' or 'What am I not seeing, for this fellow human being to think so differently to me?'

Rapport – being in the dance

I love this one – I think of it as the dance. And for me the closest thing to heaven is dancing.

I am sure that you like some people and don't like others. But have you worked out why that is? Often one of the things that has an impact on whether you like someone or not is whether you are able to be in rapport.

Over the years, I have been really fascinated by the dance we do with others. I don't mean the dance you might do on a dance floor. I am talking about a subtle dance you do when you are with people. We naturally and unconsciously try to get into their rhythm.

When we are not in the dance, things feel awkward, we are prone to disagreeing and can even dislike someone without knowing why.

This is rapport at play. Rapport means having a good understanding of someone and an ability to communicate well with them. It's a fascinating subject – and it's key if you want to get on with people. It is so much easier to influence people if you have rapport with them.

I remember a situation where I wanted to collaborate with another coach, but we just couldn't get on. She was so very different to me. I didn't realise it then, but I just couldn't get into the rhythm of her dance.

She was someone who spoke and did things really slowly. I'm pretty much the opposite of that; I speak and do things quickly. Neither was right or wrong. We were just different, and I just couldn't– however hard I tried– get into her dance. Consequently, we ended up having quite a brave conversation and decided to go our own ways and not collaborate. If only I had known more about rapport at that time, then I might have been able to salvage the situation and do some productive work with her.

Having done much work around this, I can share with you the component parts of the dance.

If you have ever watched a loving couple having dinner at a restaurant, or a pair of best friends, you will likely observe the most beautiful dance. They match and mirror their loved one's behaviours without even realising it. And in the process of this beautifully coordinated dance, they feel truly connected and listened to.

They are likely to have similar:

- Posture

- Gestures

- Breathing

- Energy levels

- Language

- Speech patterns

- Tonality

- Beliefs

- Values.

Knowing that people feel connected when others are in a subtle dance with them is such useful information. If you want to get on with someone (a new boss, partner, colleague, friend), making the effort to be in their dance can make all the difference.

I am not suggesting you should mimic them to the point of irritation or lose your own personality; what I am saying is *try it* to see what a powerful difference it can make.

The next time you're in a meeting with someone, become super observant. Watch how they breathe, and notice how quickly or slowly they speak, how they sit, how they walk, and what their favourite phrases or sayings are.

When you increase your sensory acuity (the words that describe this level of observation), you can easily choose to step into the dance.

> *"When we like someone, we are*
> *more receptive to their ideas."*
>
> **ROBERT CIALDINI**

I would even go a step further: when we *are like* someone, they are more receptive to our ideas.

If there is someone in your life that you don't see eye to eye with, using your sensory acuity and choosing to get into rapport with them can be a potent way of changing the relationship. Without changing your message in any way, if you choose to get into rapport with this person they will somehow feel differently towards you, without realising why.

When you actively listen and are in rapport with someone, you will find that you have more in common than you think, and that you are in a completely different state to negotiate any remaining differences. Don't just take my word for it; get out there and have a go.

THRIVE toolkit exercise:
rapport

Think of your list of target relationships from the earlier section and choose someone with whom you don't yet see eye to eye.

Have you got that person in mind? Good!

Now, write down in your journal all the attributes that you have noticed about them during your previous interactions:

- Do they sit upright or slouch?

- Do they speak fast or slow?

- What about their tonality?

- High or low pitch?

- Smooth or staccato?

- Do they pause a lot, or is it hard to spot when they take a breath?

- Do they keep eye contact or are they prone to look away?

- What about their breathing? Is it fast and shallow or deep and slow?

- Are they a high-energy person or a low-energy person?

Gather as many facts as you can from your memory.

Now think about yourself. What are the biggest differences between your target person and yourself? Perhaps it's the way you speak, or the way you tend to sit, or your energy level.

Whatever it is, think about something you could do differently to get more into their dance. Don't worry – you are not going to have to change what you say or your personality along the way. Think of this as an experiment. It's not a life commitment, just something you can try out to see what impact it has.

And if you have a few tricky characters in your environment, you don't need to change your 'work you'. We're talking about small nuances in specific situations right now.

Now you have decided what the biggest differences are and what you could do differently, jot them down in your journal and bear them in mind when you next interact. Don't worry if it's not a face-to-face meeting; this can work just as well virtually or even over the phone.

Once the meeting is complete, reflect on what was different. Did you feel different? Did you get a different response from the other person? Jot down anything and everything that you noticed.

Decide what you will do again that worked, and think about what else you could do to increase your level of rapport with this person the next time you interact with them.

Seeing is believing. Keep practising this skill in every interaction you have. Having good rapport skills is a must for successful, high-performance individuals.

The other thing to be aware of is that being out of rapport is also a useful strategy on occasion. You might have noticed this unconsciously before. For example, when someone wants to wrap up a meeting, they may look at their watch, start putting their papers away or grab their jacket. These are all subtle ways of breaking rapport and making it easier to finish up.

Remember this when you need to disagree with someone. Deliberately resisting getting into rapport or breaking rapport will make it easier for you to maintain a different point of view.

Agreements avoid disagreements

If only I had known about this one! Of course, the phrase 'agreements avoid disagreements' seems obvious, but the question is: do *you* have clear agreements, or are many of your relationship interactions ambiguous?

Are you making assumptions about what is being requested without checking the real meaning?

Are you taking what you know and running with it for fear of upsetting someone by asking for more clarity? Maybe you think you should have understood, and you don't want to ask again for fear of appearing stupid.

I have done all of those things over the years, and it has cost me dearly.

Personal story:
if only I had been brave and asked

I remember one incident that I am not proud of. I was working at Goldman Sachs at the time; one of the partners asked me quite casually in a meeting on Friday afternoon whether I could get some information together for him for Monday morning.

It was quite a bit of work but, instead of pushing back and seeking further clarification of exactly what he wanted, I went back to my team and told them their weekend was cancelled because we needed to get this task done.

I had picked up on a throwaway comment and run with it. Have you ever done that? Been so eager and willing to please that you didn't take stock and ask the sensible questions? When I look back, it was crazy.

My team were not happy. One of them, Nigel, had recently got engaged; I remember to this day when his fiancée came into the office on Saturday and told me what she thought of me in her broad, colourful, Irish way. It wasn't pretty, but I really don't blame her.

As it turned out, we managed to get the task done. I proudly went up to the partner first thing on Monday morning to present the report – only to be told, 'Thank you, but you shouldn't have gone to so much trouble. I was only mildly curious – it wasn't important.'

Oh my God – what an idiot I was not to have a better conversation with him to get clear on what he wanted and why! If I'd had the courage to do that, we would have worked out that it wasn't the right thing to do and we wouldn't have wasted valuable time producing something that wasn't necessary. The team would have had the weekend off that they deserved.

So many people operate their whole lives without ever checking their assumptions, and it causes all sorts of frustrations and disagreements. For example, a husband and wife who each assume their spouse will do all the jobs their father and mother did – putting out the rubbish, for example, or sewing on a button. Never once has it been explicitly agreed, but somehow these unspoken contracts exist and then cause potentially huge disagreements when things don't go according to plan.

How many assumptions are you operating under?

As soon as you start thinking about it, you will probably realise there are many stuck rigidly in place. Hundreds, even. Now, you might not want to make all of them explicit, but I bet there are one or two that have caused you niggles in the past and which would be worth having a conversation about.

Whether that is at home or at work, keep in mind the mantra: agreements avoid disagreements. I had a lovely partner once who used to drive me crazy by saying things like 'I'm just off to pick up a paper' and then disappearing for a couple of hours. I didn't know whether I should worry and send out a search party, or chill out (not my style) and hang loose.

My expectation was that he'd be half an hour max; when he wasn't back two hours later, I felt pissed off having to ring his mobile to see if he was OK. His response was always the same: 'Oh… I thought I'd go for a walk while I was at it.'

I would feel annoyed. If I'd known this was the plan, I would probably have joined him – or, if he didn't want me to, I would have settled myself into something else and not worried. I can hear some of you cry, you sound like a control freak. But it's not that (well, maybe it is!). It's just that certainty really matters to me.

I am up for changing plans. For me it's important that those changes are communicated to me, so I don't have to consume energy worrying. I try to conserve my energy for the things that matter.

I am sure you have been let down at the last minute at home or at work at some point, and you wished someone had just had the courage to tell you about the change in their plans earlier on. Getting that agreement is important; if someone doesn't know what's important to you, they can't make a choice for themselves: to act or not to act!

SURVIVE toolkit exercise:
agreements

What have you got going on in your life at work or home that is ambiguous and unclear? Perhaps there is something you feel obliged to do but you don't understand why or how. Possibly there is a task you have been asked to do, but you know someone else is already doing it, or something similar, and it's going to be awkward to go ahead.

What I want you to do right now is to jot down anything that comes to mind that is giving you a negative niggle. Don't hold back. Everything and anything you can think of fits the bill and could be jotted down.

Six pillars to influence

All the things in this section affect your ability to influence others. But there are a few more that are also important. These ideas come from the work of Robert Cialdini, where he talks about six pillars to influence.[25]

Most of these ideas will make sense to you, but you may not have thought about consciously using them when you want to have impact or influence. Combining these ideas together and having them as part of your strategy when you really need to influence can make all the difference.

What are the six pillars?

- **Likeness/rapport**: we discussed this earlier. When we like someone (or *are like* someone), we are more receptive to their ideas. If we don't like someone, we are quick to judge and shut down. Use likeness and rapport as a tool in your interactions.

- **Scarcity**: if something is scarce, we automatically

have a desire for it, as was brilliantly shown through the UK's panic buying of loo rolls early in the pandemic. If you are trying to influence people to take some action, and if there is a limited supply or limited time, that is an effective way to get people to act.

For example, maybe there's something you want to implement but you're not getting the approvals you need as swiftly as you would like. By pointing out the limited time remaining before year end, or a regulation change, that could help nudge people into action.

- **Authority**: most of us are susceptible to this one. If the most senior person in your organisation asked you to do something, you would probably be more inclined to bend over backwards to fulfil the request than if someone below you in the hierarchy had asked.

- **Consistency**: when you're trying to influence people, consider whether your message is aligned and consistent with their current thinking. If it is, and it's just an extension of the current situation, you will find it easier to influence them. If it is something new and outside their current understanding, then it's going to be much harder. Go with the things that are consistent first to reassure your audience before sharing the new ideas.

- **Consensus**: humans often have a herd mentality, which is useful to know when presenting your ideas. If you can say that your competitors are doing it, or most of the industry is on board, then the chances are others will follow. The same is true around a boardroom table or committee. If most people are already on board, it's easier to persuade the others.

- **Reciprocity**: I find this last one the most interesting – not because it's a surprise to me, but because of its lasting impact. This is all about doing something for someone else so they feel more inclined to do something for you.

You know what it's like: if someone buys you a drink, you feel obliged to repay the gesture and get the next round. The same is true in the business world, and in life in general. If you do something for someone else, you can more easily reach out when you want a favour in return. The good news here is that you can continually go out of your way to make gestures of goodwill, knowing they will be repaid at some point in the future. This concept can last eons. They can even be passed down generations before they are repaid. Just keep doing good turns, because you never know when you will need to ask a favour.

THRIVE toolkit exercise:
influence

When is the next time you'll need to influence someone, at home or at work?

Write down ideas against all the six pillars of influence mentioned above:

- How could you get into rapport with this person?

- Is there a way of sharing scarcity to encourage action?

- What about authority – how might this key be used?

- What is the current thinking, and is it consistent with your idea? How could you pull out elements to show consistency?

- Who is already doing this? Who is already on board? How will you share that there is already consensus?

- What could you do now to help the other person? Or what favour could you call upon to get this done?

Remember to document how the interaction went afterwards. Did you have more success than you have had in the past? Use WWW.EBI (What Went Well, and what would be Even Better If).

Courageous conversations

What comes to mind when you consider courageous conversations?

Some people just can't face the prospect and avoid them at all costs. The problem with doing that is they find it very difficult to be at peace with the other person; they get stuck, don't know how to proceed, and often harbour a sense of resentment. And this can go on for years.

Ask me how I know!

And what do these all-consuming thoughts and resentments do? They cause dis-ease, literally – they make you sick.

The answer is, of course, to put on your 'big girl pants' and just have the conversation. And the good news is that, after the initial discomfort, there's clarity: at least you now know the other person's point of view rather than imagining the worst. You will gain a sense of peace, and you can finally move forward.

Over the years, I have agonised over certain conversations for months – and every time, the outcome was nothing like I had feared. If only I had been brave enough to have the conversations earlier, I would have saved a lot of angst.

Personal story:
my lodger Helen

Only last night, my 24-year-old lodger, Helen, said over dinner, 'Could we have a courageous conversation?' This was music to my ears; I know it would have taken a lot for her to pluck up the courage to utter those words.

I became curious and slightly anxious as I wasn't sure what she had on her mind, but I was also excited to find out. In the past, I might have immediately gone into defensive mode and prepared myself for battle. But I have come a long way; I'm proud of myself.

It's never as bad as you imagine.

What my niece wanted to talk about was that she had accidentally caused damage to a mirror and the carpet in her bedroom; she knew I really looked after my possessions, and she was feeling very guilty.

To be honest, I had noticed it and had been feeling a bit pissed off that she'd marked the carpet and broken the mirror, but I hadn't said anything and was waiting for a time to speak to her about it. I was so pleased that she reached out first. It made all the difference.

Feedback

Having a 'courageous conversation' is not the only thing people worry about and avoid. The other biggy is feedback – both giving and receiving!

Have you ever found yourself dreading having to give someone feedback? You know something needs to be said but you worry about what to say and how and when to say it.

It may be giving you sleepless nights; you toss and turn, going through the scenario time and time again and imagining the worst. Perhaps you keep postponing the meeting for fear of the other person's response, so it's still hanging over you.

It's horrid. I have to say, I have done far too much agonising over giving feedback in my time. I decided a few years ago that I'd had enough! I didn't want to keep living my life this way.

Most people struggle with giving feedback, because we don't like upsetting others. Much of that feeling probably originates from our childhood, when feedback from teachers or parents might have been a telling off, or worse.

Feedback has negative connotations of bad news and things you don't want to hear. But is that really true? Does it have to be so?

I can't remember exactly when it was, but someone said to me a few years ago that feedback was a gift. You could withhold this gift so that the person never knew how you felt and how their behaviour was affecting others, or you could share it with them so they had some choice about what to do next.

This reframing changed everything. I now use my courageous conversation skills to give away 'gifts' all the time. The trick is to give feedback that doesn't make the other person squirm.

The key to giving feedback is to follow a simple formula.

Remember that feedback is only helpful if it is timely. It's no good sharing feedback with someone about something that happened months or even years ago. They won't remember it like you do, and you could find yourself disputing the facts. Don't leave it. If you need or want to give feedback, do it as soon as you can.

Set yourself up for success

Don't just launch into feedback with someone. Give them a choice about when you'll get together to speak. You might want to say something like: 'I have some feedback for you– when would be a good time to sit down and share it?

People don't like incompletion. You will probably find that the person will want to have the conversation sooner rather than later, so they don't have to live in suspense.

After you have agreed a time, consider the environment. Choose somewhere private and neutral. An office or meeting room? Or perhaps you could walk around a park?

Be clear about what you want to say. Make it specific and share the impact it had on you. It is wise to do the same for both positive and negative feedback.

Positive feedback

Share what they did very specifically, rather than by using general platitudes like 'Great call!' For example: 'When you completed that report on time, I noticed that everyone had time to read it and raise more questions, and so there was a useful debate. I was proud of your contribution.'

This makes it specific and actionable, so they can repeat the behaviours that went well the next time.

Negative feedback

Share what they did – again, very specifically, not as general platitudes. This means they know precisely what not to do next time. Share the impact and your personal response.

For example: 'When you handed that report in with typos in it, I noticed how disappointed I felt. For me accuracy is important, so it's important to me that you produce reports that I can feel confident can be distributed.

Then share what they can do differently next time (using 'future language' rather than describing what they did wrong or ineffectively, because they can't change the past). Again, make it specific enough so that they know exactly what to do differently next time. Share what the benefit of their future behaviour would be.

For example: 'Next time, I'd like you to take the time to review the document and run a spell check. In that way, we can both feel confident that reports can be distributed which will accurately reflect the quality of the work we produce.'

Once you have got into the habit of delivering feedback in this way– and it will take some practice– you will be amazed how differently you feel about giving and possibly even receiving future feedback. It sure is a gift.

THRIVE toolkit exercise:
giving feedback

In your journal, write down the names of all the people you would like to give feedback to. Positive and negative feedback, at home and at work. Family, friends, work colleagues, bosses. Write them all down.

Now review your list. Choose someone you want to give positive feedback to and someone to whom you need to give negative feedback. Think of it as an opportunity to practise. I suggest you start with small steps.

Think about what you want to say in each of these scenarios. What, specifically, do you want to give feedback about? The more specific you can be, the better. Write it down.

Next, reflect and consider what impact the situation had on you. If you own it, they can't dispute it. If you say something like 'So-and-so said you didn't handle that last board meeting very well' or 'You did that wrong', that won't work. It can easily be disputed, and you are not being specific.

Instead say something like, 'When you raised your voice in that last board meeting, I felt embarrassed. I wasn't able to concentrate on what you were saying and so I didn't understand the point you were trying to make.'

The next step is to get yourself ready. How can you be your best self when you are giving this gift?

Make sure you have planned it, and that you have plenty of time and don't feel rushed. How can you get into rapport with this person based on experience? Now JFDI! Don't dilly-dally. Get out there and have a go.

And report back. Remember WWW.EBI – what worked well and what would be even better if...? Whatever the outcome, congratulate yourself for having a courageous conversation and giving the gift of feedback.

What about conversations with friends or loved ones?

Step 2: Contributing to others

Having impact and influence clearly matters, but it's not the only thing…

I have noticed that the successful people who don't burn out seem to have a 'service' mindset: they want to make a difference to the people around them.

You might ask whether that really happens in the cut-throat corporate world of professional services? My belief, based on my experience, is *yes*.

You might also be thinking, 'Those people clearly have a lot more free time than I do!' But the thing is that it's not about time; it's the attitude that makes the difference.

The drug to be addicted to

Does contribution matter? Can't we be just as successful without having to also worry about 'the greater good'? There are probably people in your world who do just that and seem to be successful.

But I believe contribution is one of the magic ingredients of life.

Cast your mind back to a time when you did a good deed for someone. It could be as simple as helping someone across the road or picking up some shopping for a neighbour. What about the time when you went out of your way to get that 'special something' for someone who matters to you? I am sure you can think of plenty of examples.

Remember how good it felt. That's because of oxytocin – the 'happy hormone'. Oxytocin is addictive. Yes, you read that right: this feel-good happy hormone is addictive. Isn't that amazing? Nature makes it feel good to do things for others. And so we want to go out there and do more good deeds.

Oxytocin is also a natural stress reduction hormone. It encourages your blood vessels to dilate, which automatically brings down your blood pressure and lowers your feelings of stress.

Awesome! Doing good in the world is not only good for others – it's good for you too!

SURVIVE toolkit exercise:
creating the happy hormone!

Please open your journal and jot down your ideas for answering these questions.

- How can I be of service to others today?

- What good deed (however big or small) could I do today?

- Who in my network needs a good deed right now?

- Who's done a good deed for me that I would like to recognise and thank?

Notice now how different you feel when you consider doing a good deed for others. That's the happy hormone at work – don't you just love it?

Finding your meaning

I believe you don't have to change your job or situation to get a sense of meaning. I genuinely believe that to be true.

My experience has shown me that, provided you are honouring your values on a day-to-day basis, then you are aligned with who you are, and that brings fulfilment and meaning.

The question is: are you living in alignment? Let's see this idea in action.

Client story:
Lisa, aligning to her values

Lisa, one of my executive coaching clients, did the values exercise in Chapter 4 and found that freedom and honesty were top of her list. She had been feeling wretched and compromised in her role and couldn't see a way out, other than leaving. Her boss was a control freak who didn't allow her the autonomy she wanted, and she felt she was working in an environment that did not practise honesty.

Everything was ambiguous, which Lisa felt meant her boss could change her mind and manipulate the situation whenever the fancy took her. It was doing Lisa in, and she was on the verge of giving up. I encouraged her to try out another strategy before she made that move.

From the stories she told me, I knew that getting out and hiking in the hills of Scotland, where she lived, was very important to her; it gave her that sense of freedom, but right now she wasn't doing it. She felt worn down and didn't have the energy or inclination.

The other thing I noticed about her in our work together was that Lisa was swift to dismiss the way she felt. She wasn't really being honest with herself about what was going on and the impact it was having on her mood and wellbeing. She was a bit shocked when I pointed this out – all the more so because being honest (including with herself) was one of her top values.

I asked her, 'What if nothing else changed except that you got out into the Scottish hills at the weekends to enjoy some freedom, and you started a journal about how you are really feeling?'

Despite her belief that it wouldn't change anything, because the problem clearly lay with her boss, she agreed to give it a go.

Lisa was rather bashful when we next met because she couldn't believe what a difference it had made. Getting that uplifting freedom fix at the weekends had made it much easier to tackle the week ahead. And by journaling her feelings honestly, she felt less burdened.

'Great,' I said, 'but how are things with your controlling boss?'

'Oh, so much better! Nothing has fundamentally changed, but I'm not reacting to it in the same way.'

The moral of this story is that if you don't feel like you have meaning in your life right now, get aligned with your values and start to live them every day. You can't just take my word on this; you need to get out there and try it for yourself.

THRIVE toolkit exercise:
finding your meaning

Grab your journal and look back at the exercise you did about your values (Chapter 4).

1. Ask yourself: how much meaning do I feel I have in my life right now?

Score it out of 10, where 10 is the maximum amount of meaning.

2. Next, write down your top five values from the earlier exercise.

3. Update your scores for each value, asking yourself (out of 10) whether you are living this value right now.

4. How could you bring more of these values to life in your job?

5. How are you spending your money? Does your spending reflect your values?

6. How are you spending your time? Does your use of time reflect your values?

7. What could you do in these three areas (actions, money, time) to honour your values better?

8. Spend the next three weeks intentionally demonstrating these values in your work, whether it is with your actions, money or time.

9. Jot down what changed as a result of you living your values. After three weeks, note again how you are feeling.

10. On a scale of 1–10, how much meaning do you feel you have in your life now?

Inspired by David Tapnack, Partner and Mental Health Advocate, PwC.

Aligning with a purpose

"He who has a why for life can bear any how."

FRIEDRICH NIETZSCHE

One of the key resilience practices I know is the process of aligning with a purpose. And you don't have to take yourself off to a far-flung retreat to meditate for a month or two to discover your life purpose – although I understand that works for some. Nor am I suggesting that you chuck in your job to find your purpose.

What I am suggesting, however, is that by aligning to a purpose, you will find it much easier to stay resilient and have the energy and enthusiasm to go the extra mile. The way ahead becomes clearer, decisions are easier, and you will feel less overwhelmed with everything you have on your plate.

When you connect what you do to why it matters to you and others, you will find a source of energy that can sustain you.

Take the janitor to whom President John F Kennedy introduced himself on a visit to NASA in 1961. The janitor was mopping the floor, and the president asked him what he was doing at NASA. The janitor replied, 'Sir, I'm helping put a man on the moon.'

As this short story illustrates, the janitor was in no doubt that his contribution mattered. That's what I want for you too!

I want you to know that your contribution matters despite whatever is going on around you. This knowledge comes when you align what you are doing to something bigger that will serve others.

Depending on what sort of organisation you work for, you might not even know what your company's mission or vision is, and that might mean you feel disconnected from it. I see that quite often when I'm working with corporate clients.

But don't let this get in the way. It is still possible. You will get a boost of energy and clarity when you align with something bigger that serves others. For example, perhaps you know that developing and bringing on the younger people in your organisation matters to you. With that knowledge, you can treat each interaction differently, stepping into the role of mentor or role model to honour that value.

Client story:
Sumit, serving the underprivileged

One of my senior banking clients, Sumit, was having a tough time of it. He hadn't got the promotion he felt he deserved, and his boss always seemed to find fault. When I started working with him, he was seriously looking for a way out and had started to interview with other firms.

In the course of our work together I asked him what was important to him, and the thing that came out strongly every time we spoke was his determination to help the underprivileged. I asked him, 'How does working for this organisation allow you to serve the underprivileged?'

Immediately he came to life, as he described the internal project he had spearheaded that supported a local school with a lot of underprivileged kids. Not only had he managed to raise a considerable amount of money, which the organisation had matched, but he had also commandeered his colleagues to give up a day every so often to go into the school and support these children.

When he thought about moving on and what would happen to this project, he quickly realised that he wanted to ensure those kids continued to be supported, so he needed to hang around.

I'm pleased to say that he did stay at that organisation and, with some coaching support, got the promotion he deserved. By sticking with it and supporting the cause that was important to him, Sumit was able to tap into a source of energy that enabled him to stay on and have purpose.

Tapping into this source of immense power can reignite or sustain our desire to keep going when it could be easier to give up.

I was a guest speaker at an infertility clinic away day recently and was really taken by how the attendees came alive when they tapped into why they were doing what they were doing: helping to create families. By tapping into their clients' stories and seeing and hearing about how their work was not only creating life but changing the lives of the would-be parents, they became reignited. When groups of people connect with a collective purpose like this, extraordinary results can happen.

Viktor Frankl talks about this very subject in his book *Man's Search for Meaning.* His theory was that meaning was a central human motivational force and that people would be more likely to survive the concentration camps if they visualised themselves doing something positive after the horror was over. Frankl himself imagined his own future – after his release – giving lectures and helping others understand what it was like in these camps.

We can all tap into this driving force, but how? Particularly when things are tough, how do we do that?

The best way I know is to keep asking the question, 'What matters to me and how will this serve others?' Keep asking; when you get there, you'll know. There will be a different energy about you. You'll feel invigorated and decisive, bold, strong and clear. There'll be a confidence about you that others will witness. Instead of wanting to give up, you will want to give your all.

THRIVE toolkit exercise:
looking for purpose

Write down the answers to these questions:

- What really matters to you?

- What makes you come alive?

- What inspires you?

- Step into your future, 10 years from now; what will be important to you at that stage of your life?

- What do you want to be remembered for?

- What do you want to contribute to the world?

- What do you want someone to say in your eulogy?

Summary of OTHERS

Clearly, mastering your SELF and mastering TIME would not be enough on their own; you need to be able to master your relationship with OTHERS too.

In this chapter you have learnt:

Step 1: Communicating with others

The importance of:

▶ First seeking to understand

▶ Listening

▶ Rapport

▶ Agreements; they avoid disagreements

▶ How to influence

▶ Courageous conversations.

Step 2: Contributing to others

The importance of:

▶ Making a difference to others

▶ Finding your meaning

▶ Aligning to a purpose

And added the following tools to your toolkit:

SURVIVE (QUICK) TOOLKIT	THRIVE TOOLKIT
STEP 1: COMMUNICATING WITH OTHERS	
Agreements	Understanding your relationships
	Active listening
	Rapport
	Influence
	Giving feedback
STEP 2: CONTRIBUTING TO OTHERS	
Creating the happy hormone	Finding your meaning
	Looking for purpose

CHAPTER 7

PERFORMANCE

*"The goal is not to be better than the other man,
but your previous self."*

DALAI LAMA XIV

What is the PERFORMANCE step all about?

Even if you understand yourself, managing also to master time and influence others, those things on their own won't necessarily mean you are going to be successful. You might not burn out, but have you set yourself up for success?

Not necessarily. You need this last piece in the puzzle – a sustainable optimal performance strategy.

The PERFORMANCE step is all about your sustainable long-term high performance – not peaks followed by episodes of burnout, but a sustainable way of working that works for you.

In this chapter I will share key strategies for making better choices, and ways to set yourself up for long-term success so that you can reap the rewards of a career and life well spent.

Why is the PERFORMANCE step important?

If you don't have a PERFORMANCE mindset and habits, the chances are you will throw yourself into your career with no long-term plan in mind. You may do well early on because of your enthusiasm and work ethic but then find you can't keep up the pace.

Thrivers pride themselves on making better choices in terms of the way they live their lives. They choose wisely, with the long term in mind. When you do this, it changes your attitude toward short-term decision-making and really focuses your mind on your sustainable high performance.

This 'living on purpose' has a profound impact on your potency and sense of freedom – something many others don't enjoy. It's a mindset shift. It requires you to have a strategic approach to your career and wellbeing, and has positive knock-on effects for all aspects of your life.

As you know by now, it can take years to recover if you burn out, and you will never get back that vital, productive and financially lucrative time again – the time when your career is on fire and you progress beyond your expectations. Your future life will always be impacted by your short-sightedness if you don't get this right. I am not saying that to be cruel or sensationalist; I am saying it to give you a gentle warning that your long-term future is in your hands and only *you* can do anything about it.

What happens when you overlook PERFORMANCE?

Client story:
Annabel, making sacrifices

Let me tell you about Annabel. She worked for a well-known investment bank and loved the 'work hard, play hard' environment she found herself in. She was doing rather well in her early thirties but worked extremely hard, working all the hours God sent. She sacrificed her relationships and her fertile years to please others and to earn an excellent salary. She couldn't keep it up, though, and she burnt out.

That was then. Now she is in her sixties. She tried but didn't have the stuffing to return to the investment banking world, so lost out on years of good salary, bonus, and pension while she did her best to recover. She did go back to work a few years later but found it difficult to cope with any stressful situation and, as we know, all jobs are stressful at times.

She now has a job that pays her less than a quarter of what she earned 25 years ago, doesn't have enough of a pension to fall back on and is looking at a future that's rather grim. She knows she needs to keep working to pay her bills, but is weary and tired, lonely, and regretful.

I really don't want Annabel's story to be your story.

You might be thinking, 'That's not going to happen to me. I can't see myself not being able to work and earn a good salary.' But the thing is, nor could she. She ignored the signs, missed out on some key years and has never been able to get back on track.

You also might be thinking, 'Surely she could get a better job than the one she currently has.' Well, that's probably true, but she's not the woman she was. She only has a limited time to sort it out, and she's not sure she has it in her.

But it doesn't need to be this way. Read on to learn about some key strategies that will make all the difference.

Step 1: Making better choices

To have a high-performance strategy for the long term, you need to make good choices. Daily choices and subsequent actions add up over time and get you to where you are. So ask yourself, are the choices you are making day in and day out going to get you to where you want to be? The chances are, unless you have your high performance in mind, that they will not.

Perhaps you're choosing to postpone things like going to the gym or getting enough sleep. Yet we know tomorrow never comes and you can't wind the clock back. Perhaps you keep on pushing through, hoping for the best.

If that's the case, the reality is that you need to make better choices. Not the big fat hairy choices; the day-to-day decisions, the micro-decisions you make that nudge the needle in the right direction and improve your ability to perform at a high level for the long term.

We're all pushing ourselves these days, trying to get more done in less time, using technology to help us. But the thing is, *is it sustainable*? Can you really continue to push yourself like this and expect to be on peak form in three, five, ten years down the line?

I suspect not.

And literally no one else can do this for you. You can't delegate your sleep or fitness to someone else. Only you can do these things, so the choice is yours. Are your daily habits moving you towards or away from what you want? Are the small daily habits nudging you towards a better place over time?

It's a bit like being at the controls of a giant container ship, the kind that you can only imagine falling over in a big sea. If you ever see these ships turn a corner, you will notice that they must do it slowly.

They are not the sort of vehicle that can turn on a six-pence – quite the opposite. The captain at the wheel will be moving it only slightly, but knows full well that he will turn the corner for sure if he maintains his course and keeps going.

That's the same for us. If we keep making better choices, over time our situation will improve, and we can create a sustainable way of working that will give us the results we want. Nothing drastic – just small choices that will ultimately help you turn the corner and get you on your way. Sounds simple, doesn't it? But how do you do it?

"What did cause me stress was doing more and more and picking up more and more people's jobs and roles without support. I was on 24/7. My brain

was never switched off. I had young kids, so I would take weekends off to do all those things you do, Legoland and Disney World. But looking back, I'm not sure I was ever that present. My mind was always at work, even if my body and consciousness wasn't. I think about 50% of the pressure lifted when I found out that I was one of many, rather than it was just me. Looking back, I realise how stressful work was for about 10 years.

"It does take its toll. First, I started struggling to sleep. And then it moved from anxiety to depression; I was feeling low and scared, as it was there all of the time, and at the weekends I wasn't recharging."

PERRY BURTON, HEAD OF PEOPLE AND CULTURE, GRANT THORNTON UK LLP

Have long-term high performance in mind

The first step in making better choices is to have your long-term high performance in mind – *really* in mind. Thinking, every day, 'Is what I am doing helping or damaging me in the long term?' Having this mindset means you automatically make better choices and can't ignore the choices you make that are not serving you.

Let me give you a current and very personal example. I have COVID-19 in the house right now and I ought to be doing everything I can to keep myself healthy to stave off any potential infection.

Last night, having spent the last four days locked in, and doing an average of only 3,000 steps a day, I was going a bit stir crazy and decided to treat myself to a glass of red wine. In fact, two glasses of red wine. Not the end of the world, you might say. You deserve a pick-me-up, under the circumstances.

But the thing is, I have noticed over the last few years that every time I drink red wine, I sleep badly— and, sure enough, I had a rotten night's sleep. Not what I needed if I wanted to keep my immunity up.

I made a bad choice. One that clearly didn't serve me.

Tonight, if I need a pick-me-up (and I am not recommending drinking every night) then a G&T or a glass of white wine will be a better choice. The reality is that 'treat' was just a way of 'treating myself badly'.

So how will I help myself when the time comes? Well, I have thrown out the remainder of the red and I have put a yellow Post-it on the glasses cupboard door to remind me to make a better choice— ideally, not to drink alcohol at all.

Instead of a Post-it, you could write a note in your diary at the beginning of each day that says, 'Make better choices'. You could have a daily reminder in your electronic diary or hand-write it in your physical diary.

Or you could have a picture or memento that reminds you of, or symbolises, your ideal thriving self. I have a picture of an older woman, looking great and agile on a lovely looking boat, as my screen saver. Or you could have a physical object like a picture or an ornament. Each time you look at this item, it anchors you into your ideal future and helps you make better choices now.

What nudge do you need to create to remind yourself that your long-term high performance matters?

Being outcome-orientated

I am always surprised at the number of people who, when I ask them about what they want, respond by telling me everything they don't want. It's a completely different question, guys! But what's the harm in that? Actually, quite a bit!

Let me tell you about a particular part of the brain called the reticular activating system. This part of the brain is known for (amongst other things) filtering what you see and experience. You might have experienced its effects when you have bought a new car. Before you bought it, you hardly saw any of that particular make and model in that colour– but now, you see them everywhere. They were there before, of course, but you just didn't notice them. Whatever you think about, you see out there in the world.

By telling yourself about all the things you don't want, guess what you will be seeing and attracting?

Now, maybe you don't believe in all this 'woo-woo' stuff, and besides, maybe you don't actually know what you want, exactly. All you know is that you don't want what you've got right now.

Maybe you're single and you don't want to be single. I get it; I am single right now and don't want to be. I could spend my energy and focus on what I don't want but instead, I am thinking about the man I do want in my life. What he might look like, his qualities, what adventures we might go on together, where I'd like to live with him, how we'll deal with differences, what sports and hobbies we'll enjoy, and so on. I would recommend you do the same.

Being outcome focused stops you attracting what you don't want, but it also energises you towards what you do want.

The same is true in the work context. If you have a challenging project that is not going according to plan, the worst thing you can do is to focus all your attention on what's not working. Of course, you need to mitigate risks and ensure that what's going wrong is minimised and isn't going to completely derail the situation. But once you've done that, your focus needs to be the outcome. Keep an eye on the prize.

Client story:
Lee, focusing on the outcome

Let me give you an example. Lee, a client of mine, was leading a very high-profile IT project in his company. It was not going well. It was looking less and less likely to hit the deadline, and that would have major financial consequences for the company.

His bosses were on his case, and Lee was beginning to question whether he was the right man for the project. In a coaching session, he was totally consumed with what was going wrong. Every thought he had was about what was not working, all the problems he and his team had, and the consequences of the project failing for customers, shareholders, the management team, and himself and his team.

He was using all his time and energy on the problem and what was going wrong.

Instead of allowing Lee to sit there wallowing in the situation, I decided to do something that would change his state of mind and help him to think differently. I suggested that we went for a walk instead of staying in the poky coaching room. I told him that to be able to see things differently, he had to agree to keep his head up to encourage blue-sky thinking (there's another reason I suggested that, but that's for another time).

As we walked, I asked him questions about the outcome.

Why is the outcome so important to your customers? What difference will it make to their lives? Why did your bosses choose you to lead this project? How will you feel when it's done? What has gone well, and what needs to happen now to turn this around?

What's the first step? Who could help you? What do you need to start doing, stop doing, or continue doing? What other resources do you need? How can you get them signed off? What does your team need to hear from you right now?

Within an hour, Lee had completely changed his state of mind and attitude towards the project. No longer was he doubting himself and feeling helpless. He felt confident about why he had been chosen to do this job, and now had some concrete steps he needed to take as soon as this meeting was over.

Lee was now focused on the future and what he could do to get things moving.

Lee's project didn't meet the deadline – but it wasn't far off, so the financial consequences were mitigated, and he was congratulated for turning the project around.

Research has shown that when people have positive goals, their performance is improved, while the performance of those who have avoidance goals worsens.

Not surprising when you think about it; one mindset is focused on what you want like a laser beam, and the other sees what you want dispersed into the ether, giving you no guidance or energy.

The next time you find yourself fretting and worrying about a problem, use the following questions to help you move from a problem-focused to a solution-focused approach.

THRIVE toolkit exercise:
focus on the solution

- What is the outcome you want?

- How will you know when you have got there?

- What will it feel like, look like, sound like?

- What will others see?

- What needs to happen for that to happen?

- Repeat the above question until you get to some actionable steps.

- What resources do you need?

- Who could help you?

- What do you need to stop, start and continue doing?

- How will you celebrate along the way?

Decision fatigue

Have you ever started your day with the intention of getting a particular task done but, when it came around to it, you just couldn't focus or even start? It happens to everyone – 'life' can get in the way. But, if it happens frequently, you could be suffering from decision fatigue.

Decision fatigue is now a well-recognised phenomenon.

We're having to make hundreds, if not thousands, of decisions every day, from small decisions like what to eat or wear to significant decisions about a business direction, how to secure funding, or the next step in our career.

Every decision we make takes energy, and as our brains have limited capacity, our ability to make decisions diminishes as the days go on.

When we run out of decision-making power, we either make rash, reckless decisions or we stop making decisions altogether, shutting down and doing nothing.

Please don't give yourself a hard time about not focusing on that task or going to the gym; it's probably just that you have run out of decision-making juice.

You might have heard that Steve Jobs only wore jeans, a black turtleneck and sneakers every workday, to reduce the decisions he had to make. Even Albert Einstein bought several versions of the same grey suit because he didn't want to waste brainpower on choosing an outfit each morning.

And President Obama hit the gym at 7:30 every morning and wore only blue or grey suits, for the same reason. He wanted to focus his decision-making energy on important things.

Decision-making is the force that shapes our success and destiny, whether that relates to our careers, health, relationships or family. So, if you're using up energy making many insignificant decisions, it's not surprising if you don't have the capacity to make decisions about the things that really matter.

If you want to keep your performance on track and ensure you've got sufficient decision capacity for the things that matter:

- Minimise the number of decisions you have to make

- Automate as many decisions as you can

- Organise the important decisions to be made at a time when you have the most energy.

There's a lot to be said for saying, 'Sleep on it' – I suspect for this very reason.

Decision minimising tips

Below are some suggestions for minimising the decision energy drain.

INSTEAD OF THINKING:	TRY THIS INSTEAD:
Should I put some money into my pension this month?	Set up a monthly direct debit
What shall I eat?	Plan your meals for the week in advance
What should I wear today?	Set out your clothes the night before

How will I get 7–9 hours' sleep?	Agree the time you want to be in bed earlier in the day, and set an alarm for winding down and getting your gadgets on night mode

The key thing to remember is that decisions take energy, and your brain has a limited capacity so, for heaven's sake, save the brain capacity for things that matter.

Creating certainty

Would you agree that, in recent times, there has never been as much uncertainty, whether that be due to COVID-19, Brexit, or the general political situation (I am writing this in the run-up to the 2020 US election, about which there is huge worldwide anxiety).

We know that our brains don't like uncertainty and it automatically puts us in a more stressed state, and in a place where we can't access our full potential.

We can't change *the* world, but we can change *our* world by creating pockets of certainty that enable us to feel safe and bring down those stress hormones. When you have your own pockets of certainty, you feel more in control and that leads to better decision-making, more actions and therefore more results.

But how do you create your own pockets of certainty?

Here are some examples of how some of my clients have done it:

- **Helen** tidied her office space so that she knew where everything was. This helped her feel she was more on top of things and in control of her day.

- **Sam** got on top of her finances, reducing the number of accounts and credit cards she had so that her finances didn't take so much of her head space, meaning she knew where she stood. She said she found it so much easier to reduce her debt once she was brave enough to understand where she really was.

- **Peter** decided to have courageous conversations with his nearest and dearest, because agreeing who was doing what would calm and centre him. Not knowing who was organising the decorator, or who was booking the restaurant or sorting out the accommodation for a weekend away, created unnecessary uncertainty for him that wasted time and energy.

- **Harriet** decided it was time that she knew what to do in an emergency. How would she and her partner get out of the house if there was a fire? Where is the nearest A&E? If there were a leak in the house, would she know how to turn the water off? Even though she knew the chances of any of these things happening were very small, being prepared and on the front foot enabled her to significantly reduce her anxiety and sleep better at night.

This same principle can be applied at work. Whatever decisions or concerns are keeping you awake at night, being proactive and thinking about these things in advance reduces the low-level anxiety that might be running outside of your awareness and the downright panic that might set in if it happens.

Getting a will in place helped Peter feel secure in the knowledge that his family would be looked after if anything should happen to him. He had been putting off doing a will for years and he couldn't believe how much better he felt when he put his affairs in order. (By the way, I can highly recommend John Heavens at john@yourlegacysolutions.co.uk if you have been putting off this important task and need to talk to someone who really knows his stuff.)

"I clear my inbox, I clear my mind. If I don't have an organised email system I don't know where to start my day. Some days all hell breaks loose and

everything else has to be dealt with. I do my best to stay in control and I push myself to focus and make it go right."

PAT CHIN – DIRECTOR, CHIEF OF STAFF AND BUSINESS UNIT OFFICE HEAD, CITIGROUP

Client story:
Heather, unopened mail

Heather had so much unopened mail that it almost covered her kitchen table. Most of it was junk mail, of course, but there were a couple of important letters buried in the pile. She finally decided to go through the mail, throwing out the junk without even opening it, and whittling down the pile to a manageable amount. She felt so much better after that and vowed not to let it get so bad again.

It would be easy to underestimate the positive impact that these small actions have on your wellbeing and productivity, and therefore on your decision-making. Anything that creates uncertainty is an energy drain you could do without.

Seeing setbacks as opportunities

Over the years I have certainly changed my attitude towards setbacks. Any setback at Goldman Sachs was devastating to me. I wallowed in the misery of it and beat myself up for weeks if anything did not go according to plan. It took up so much head space, made me feel rotten and ruined my sleep.

I see the same response in many of my successful, super high-achieving, perfectionist clients. They set themselves such high standards that it's like a straitjacket they can never escape from.

I used to think these high standards really served me, making me stand out from the crowd as they forced me to go the extra mile and produce better work. On reflection, I am not so sure. I might have pushed myself harder to achieve, but that just led to exhaustion over time, and the amount of time I spent wallowing in my misery, consumed by my thoughts, was not helpful or productive.

These days, when things go wrong, I give myself a short time to feel miserable – it could be for the rest of the day or an indulgent 24 hours. I can't turn the clock back and change what happened, so I have a choice of feeling wretched for longer or nipping it in the bud and acknowledging what is. When my time is up, I ask myself the following questions:

- What could I learn from this situation?

- What would I do differently if I could turn the clock back?

- What impact would that have had?

- What can I do to make now better?

- What will I do next?

Mental form

It can be hard to keep track of your mental wellbeing. Pressure can build up so slowly that it's imperceptible from one day to the next but, over time, can have a massive negative impact.

One of my dear colleagues, Rob Stephenson, has come up with a way of keeping a track of your mood and wellbeing: the FormScore. You do it by asking this simple question– 'How am I today?'– and then rating yourself out of 10, where 10 is on top form.

Our mental form affects so many things. Our resilience and ability to cope. Our thoughts about the future and how we can motivate ourselves. How vulnerable we feel in our relationships or finances. And our performance is affected by our mental form. On a good day, we can cope with and achieve so much more than we can on a day when we are feeling low.

I had one of those low days yesterday, but it wasn't until I did my mental FormScore that I realised just how low I was. I scored 5/10 – low form. I was tearful and felt exhausted. Everything I wanted to tackle felt insurmountable, and I just wanted to give up.

Good job I had a call booked into the diary with a friend of mine, Carole. Although when we started our call, I was getting through tissues nineteen to the dozen, by the end of our conversation I felt so much better and knew how to get myself back on track. Even after all this time, and actively practising what I preach, I am still human!

But, unless you check in with yourself, it's very difficult to spot your mental form declining.

OK, so what do the different scores mean? Well, of course this is just a framework and not definitive in any way, but it does help if you monitor your score over time to see which direction you are heading in.

FIG 11. FORM SCORES.

SURVIVE toolkit exercise:
mental form

You could, of course, come up with your score based on gut instinct– but if you want to be more scientific about it, grab your journal and answer the following questions, with each answer being a score out of 10:

- How motivated do I feel today?

- How easy is it to do simple tasks and make decisions?

- What are my perceived energy levels?

- How well have I slept lately?

- Have I exercised well today?

- How has my diet been recently?

- How purposeful do I feel?

- How connected am I to family and friends?

- How well am I balancing stress with recovery?

- How comfortable am I about my finances right now?

Once you've done that, add your scores together and divide by 10. What is your average form score? Is it the number you would have intuitively said or not?

If it is, then using your intuition or gut instinct to respond to the question 'How are you today?' will probably serve you. If you got a different score, then I suggest, for the next few times, that you ask yourself the individual questions to get a more accurate guide.

I highly recommend that you check in with your own FormScore on a regular basis and jot down the scores and dates in your journal so you can refer to them.

Who else in your network also needs to know about the FormScore? Who are you worried about? Who do you need to ask, 'How are you today?' We all know people in our lives who have struggled at one point or another, and we all need to be making a special effort to look out for our fellow human beings.

THRIVE toolkit exercise:
mental form

- What's your FormScore today? Is that from gut instinct or answering the 10 questions?

- Is it moving in the right direction? Or do you need to take some action and get your form back on track?

- What will you do to get your score back on track if it is low?

- Who in your network (at work and at home) are you worried about? Jot down their names or initials.

- When will you reach out to them and ask, 'How are you today?'

- How could you introduce them to the idea of the FormScore?

- When will you check in again to know if they are OK?

This simple technique has been proven to help people recognise when they are not in good shape and they need to seek some support. I suspect over time it will save lives, if it hasn't already.

Once you are in the low score region, it is often difficult to reach out to others, and if that persists, it can lead to suicidal thoughts. Asking yourself these questions and ideally sharing your scores with others has proven to be a valuable intervention that can get the ball rolling towards getting your mental form back on track and a higher score.

Sign up for the FormScore app here: **www.formscore.today**

Other sources of support are:

- Your GP

- An employee assistance programme at work

- The Samaritans (call 116 123 or email jo@samaritans.org)

- The charity MIND

- A family member or friend.

Biofeedback technology

What if you could know what was really going on inside of your body and know whether your stress levels were affecting your health?

Well, biofeedback technology allows you to know that, and before long this technology will be in all wearables (it's in a lot of them already).

By gathering data on how your heart is behaving, you can find out whether you are in the stress response or in recovery. Stress only becomes a problem if you don't have enough recovery in your typical day. Over time, if you don't have the stress recovery balance in order, you can burn out or develop another form of disease.

It's great to know that there is relatively inexpensive technology out there which can give you that feedback and help you to make better choices.

However, so many people have got used to their pressurised lives that they don't think they have a problem—and it's only when they fall over, have a heart attack, plunge into a deep depression, start having panic attacks or digestive problems that don't go away, or develop diabetes, that they start to take note and do anything about it.

But it doesn't have to be that way. If you want to have a high-performance strategy, you have to be aware of the pressures you are putting yourself under and the consequences over time.

There are consequences caused by rushing around all the time and not giving yourself a moment to breathe, let alone think. You can't keep burning the candle at both ends and expect to not get your fingers burnt. Having lots of pressure and always being 'on' might feel exciting at best and a necessity at worst, but it will take its toll.

I use biofeedback technology with my clients so they can understand how their lifestyle choices and work commitments are impacting on their ability to function at their best over time.

Typically, I get them to wear a specially designed heart rate monitor for three days, which captures their biological data to know what's really going on. These are hard facts that can't be disputed, and that's what my clients say they need and want. They want to know how stressed they became in that meeting and to know whether they are getting enough recovery.

I have to say that a significant majority of my clients are not getting enough recovery in their day to sustain their current way of work and life. They are depleting their batteries over time, and that's only going to result in one thing.

For many, taking this three-day assessment is the wake-up call they need.

"I definitely wasn't sleeping. I would go to sleep because I was so exhausted, and then I'd be awake at two or three o'clock in the morning all the time.

But I still thought, well, this is just what junior partners go through.

"I'm very aware now that, if I don't have enough sleep, that is when the meltdowns will start happening. Recovery is undervalued in the professional world."

**SAM BROWN – PARTNER AND HEAD OF
PENSIONS AT HERBERT SMITH FREEHILLS**

Did you know, for example, that doing the wrong type of exercise at the wrong time of day can be detrimental to your recovery and performance? Did you know that the quality of your sleep is as important as the quantity? You can be asleep but find that your sleep is not restorative as your body is still in the stress response.

Those are the days you wake up having had the right number of hours' sleep and yet you still feel exhausted and tired.

The technology I use was developed for elite performance athletes. The designers' intention was to identify how life-style factors could improve performance at world-class levels by a fraction of 1%.

This technology has been translated into the business world with great success, helping executives know and understand how they can function at their best and create lifestyle choices that will help them have a sustainable high performance.

If you are one of those people who likes facts and figures, charts and graphs, then getting this type of life assessment is going to be for you.

It's not for the faint hearted, though. This 'wake-up call' is an invitation to take action, make different choices, and change. And change is hard, right?

To find out more:

sarah@sarahsparks.co.uk

www.sarahsparks.co.uk

Step 2: Setting yourself up for long-term success

Planning ahead – it's a marathon, not a sprint

Many people in the business world are giving their all as if they are in a sprint. However, as soon as one race is over, another one starts, and they do the same thing again and again and again.

Before I start working with them, very few of my clients have considered pacing themselves. They just give their all, day in and day out, and are surprised they feel so exhausted all the time.

I encourage them to look at the year ahead and prepare for the work demands that they already know are coming up, whether that's monthly, quarterly, or annual deadlines, project demands, regulatory changes, or even external changes like Brexit.

It soon becomes apparent that if they are going to maintain their high performance, they need to be savvy about their holidays, long weekends and workload.

One client, Claire, discovered when we did this exercise looking at her year ahead, that she literally could not do all that had been asked of her and her team. As soon as the coaching session was over, she hot-footed to her boss's office and renegotiated what she thought was possible.

But what does 'pacing yourself' really look like?

It is an individual thing, but I suggest you look at time periods, just like Claire did for the year ahead. Then look at the months, weeks and days. What commitments have you got in the next year, quarter, month or week? What do you need to let go of, or do in advance, to create less pressure later?

SURVIVE toolkit exercise:
planning ahead

Consider how you might plan your recovery ahead of time. Perhaps you could book yourself a holiday or long weekend in preparation for a busy time. Maybe you could delegate so that others take on more.

What could you do this week to pace yourself? Maybe a couple of early nights or cutting out alcohol could help? What can you do today to pace yourself? Could you go for a walk or schedule a coffee break with a friend (to make sure you take it!)?

The company you keep

> *"You are the average of the five people you spend the most time with."*
>
> **JIM ROHN**

Have you heard that saying? When I first heard anyone speak about this, I was blown away; it had never, ever crossed my mind. As I looked at the people I spent most time with, I was clear that something needed to change.

That didn't mean immediately cutting people out of my life, but it did mean I was much more conscious about who I hung out with and why.

If you hang out with people who are fearful and negative, their outlook can't help but rub off on you. The same is true for people who are positive and enthused with life. You are exposed to and pick up on their world view, values, beliefs, ambitions and energy.

I have one friend called Denise who I can't see enough of. She exudes this amazing energy and positive 'can do' attitude, only seeing joy wherever she looks. She is a great person to hang out with. It's always a blast and I walk away inspired and feeling great.

Who are you hanging out with? Are they drains or radiators (as my mother calls them)? Drains are people who make you feel literally drained after you have spent some time with them. Radiators, on the other hand, are folks who energise you.

Denise is most definitely a radiator for me!

Of course, we all have responsibilities regarding our family members and even work colleagues, but if these people are not 'radiators', you need to limit your exposure for fear of the 'drain' in them rubbing off on you.

You know what it's like. There are certain 'friends' that you need to brace yourself for and you know that hanging out with them for long is not good for you.

**SURVIVE toolkit exercise:
who are you spending time with?**

Who are the people you have spent most time with this last week? Jot their names or initials down in your journal. Was that week typical? If not, who else do you typically hang out with? Jot their names or initials down as well.

Now ask yourself: are those people 'drains' or 'radiators'?

Who else do you know who is a 'radiator' that you would like to spend more time with? Who demonstrates the person you want to become? How could you organise your timetable to be able to hang out with them more often?

If you have some 'drains' on your list, fear not! It's not the end of the world, but it is an issue you probably should do something about. How could you limit your time with them? How can you dilute the energy drain impact? Do you need an 'imaginary cloak' on to protect your energy?

As you think of the Jim Rohn quote above, what is the average of the people you hang out with, and are they helping you thrive and have a high-performance life?

Accountability partner

Committing to a life of thriving isn't easy – I know. It takes effort and daily commitment, and sometimes it's just easier to let go and not bother.

One way to stay on track is to have an accountability partner: someone you trust who you can share your experiences with honestly, with the objective of keeping yourself on track to being your best self. Someone who will call it out if they see you falling short.

Research has shown that if you share a goal out loud with someone else, the likelihood of you achieving it increases significantly. If you have an accountability partner along the way, you ramp up your chances of getting results.

Over the years I have found accountability partners hugely helpful. On some occasions I know there is no way I would have stuck to what I had committed to unless I had buddied up with someone who was keeping an eye on me.

Whether it's a buddy who will go to the gym with you or get you out for a run, having an accountability partner helps to delegate the motivation.

We are much less likely to let someone else down than we are to let ourselves off the hook.

I have had accountability partners for exercise, book writing, blog and vlog posts, and major work projects. Each time I have chosen different partners, and each time this way of being accountable has really helped me achieve when I might have given up.

Right now, I have a meditation accountability partner. I have committed to meditate every day and to send a WhatsApp message when I have done so. We keep each other on track and prod and support each other if there isn't a daily message. I am loving it.

My accountability partner, Trish, is in the US and is someone I admire hugely. I feel honoured to be working with her in this way, and I feel connected with her as we go through 'ABC' together (the American election and the transitioning to a new chapter, Brexit with all that brings, and the global impact of the Coronavirus pandemic).

Never have I needed to meditate more to keep me centred and calm, and I know it's been hugely useful and beneficial to her too.

How to identify a good accountability partner

Be clear about what you want to focus on and be accountable for. Don't make it too complicated. Apply the KISS principle (Keep It Simple, Stupid).

Look out for someone who wants to achieve something similar. If you want to be held accountable for doing some daily training towards a marathon, it's probably not a good idea to pair up with someone who has a big project to accomplish and only wants to check in weekly or monthly.

Find someone who is ideally more disciplined than you, or at least has the same level of discipline. Someone you know who will 'say what they mean' and 'mean what they say'. You don't want to be wasting time dragging along an account- ability partner who is not equally as committed as you.

Choose someone you would hate to disappoint.

Identify someone who has the time to not only stick to their goals but also to be able to commit to making the accountability calls or sending the messages. If you find that they just don't seem to be able to make time and stick to the agreed check-ins, it's probably best to let them go and find someone else.

Having an accountability partner works both ways, so you need to be willing and comfortable to hold them account- able and call them out if they are not living up to what they said they wanted. After all, you're letting them down if you don't say something to help them stay on track.

THRIVE toolkit exercise:
accountability partner

What do you want to be held accountable for? You are of course allowed to have more than one goal, but I would recommend that you don't make it complicated. Ideally it should be one goal, one accountability partner.

What have you got coming up that it would be useful to have an accountability partner for? Who do you know that would be a good accountability partner?

What would you want them to hold you accountable for? For example, meditating daily, sleeping seven hours a night, eliminating wheat from your diet, eliminating alcohol, exercising five times a week, accomplishing something every week towards your important goal?

Once you've identified the person you want to have as an accountability partner, have a conversation and agree how it will work. Is it a weekly call or message, or is a daily reminder more appropriate? When will you start? Which milestones would be good to celebrate? How will you know when to end?

As soon as you have agreed ground rules, start to watch the magic of accountability unfold.

Enduring happiness

> *"I have chosen to be happy because it is good for my health."*

VOLTAIRE

What is happiness? What is success?

Deep stuff! And too big a topic to discuss in a short chapter. But there are a couple of things I want to bring to your attention. The first is the saying 'Money doesn't bring you happiness'. I would agree with that – but with some provisos.

My experience has shown me that money hasn't brought me happiness. But I also know that having a certain amount of money allows me to worry less. The question is: what are you striving for? If it's more money, then be careful what you wish for and keep an eye out for your happiness quotient.

What I have discovered along the way is that enduringly happy people have three things in common, regardless of how much money they have. They are:

- At peace with the past

- Present to the present

- Excited about their future.

How about you?

Are you at peace with the past or is it somewhere you visit continually? Are you fretting over past mistakes, experiences or missed opportunities that you can do nothing about? How much energy are you consuming living or revisiting episodes from the past? Have you left the past in the past, or is it still present?

If you really feel like you can't yet be at peace with the past, get some support in the form of therapy or counselling. Please note that coaching isn't appropriate here; coaching is all about the future and what you want to create going forward, and it really doesn't work very well unless you can let go of the past.

Coaching really does help with the other two, though.

When it comes to getting better at being in the now, along with appreciating and being grateful for what you have, working with a coach can really help. Of course, you can make progress in this area without a coach, too— hence this book— and the first thing I'd suggest you do is to practise gratitude.

Practising gratitude every day, and even keeping a gratitude diary, can really help bring you to a place of appreciation towards what you've got regardless of whatever is going on all around you.

Client story:
Amanda, practising gratitude

I had one client, Amanda, whose life was falling apart. Her husband had gone off with a younger model, her teenage kids were giving her hell. Work was bad. She was having to sell the family home she adored, and her husband was going to be taking the beloved black Labrador that had been in the family for years.

When I met her, she wasn't feeling grateful about what she had– understandably. We talked about enduring happiness and the three aspects that made it possible, and she became determined that this period in her life was not going to get the better of her.

I remember her saying that by the end of the divorce process, she wanted the people she cared for in her life to get the best of her, not the rest of her. With that determination, she went off to get some counselling to heal some of the episodes in her past that were consuming her thoughts.

Meanwhile, the work she did with me was about the present and the future. At first, she couldn't think much about the future, but she agreed to keep a notepad beside her bed and every night write down three things she was grateful for. Initially, she found it difficult to find three things to be grateful about, but she soon got into the swing of it, choosing the simplest things that made her glow.

Here are some of the things on her list:

- Clean bed linen
- A good night's sleep (as no one was snoring next to her)
- Time for herself
- A favourite rose in her garden
- Cindy, her friend who phoned every week
- Not feeling guilty when she worked late
- Quality time with her kids, however short
- Having every other weekend child-free
- A six o'clock G&T
- Being in control of the TV remote
- Sleeping in on a Sunday
- Going to bed whenever she chose
- Leaving the kitchen untidy if she wanted to
- Having enough money to pay her bills.

Very soon, Amanda was able to find hundreds of things she was grateful for. Practising gratitude is one of the best ways of connecting to the present. I think 'present' is such a fabulous word, too, because the present really is a gift.

And yet it's so easy to step over what's happening right now and focus on what's going to happen next or worry about what's already happened.

As Jay Shetty, a British author and former monk, says, 'When you're present in gratitude, you can't be anywhere else.'

As I said, Amanda wasn't ready to think about her future at that early stage, but when she was, I helped her come up with something that excited her and put her on a path to enduring happiness. These days she is a completely different person.

She has a job she loves, working for an organisation that values and respects its employees. She has a new home that her grown-up children love to come back to. She has another black lab and a new man in her life, both of whom adore her. Amanda can't believe her luck and good fortune, but I can. She did the work!

Don't allow yourself to wallow in unhappiness. Life is too short and it's not worth it. As Amanda has shown, you can do things to turn it around by focusing on those three things. Take charge of your happiness and decide to enjoy life. You only have one.

Integrity

I don't know about you, but the COVID-19 restrictions that have come in from time to time around the UK, and which have been different around the country, have really caused me and my family to think and navigate the 'right thing to do'. It's not been easy as things are not clear cut.

For example, do I ask for a COVID-19 test even though I don't have any symptoms? At the beginning of the crisis, the government encouraged you to get a test if someone in your household had tested positive. At the time of writing, they are asking you not to do that unless you have symptoms, so they can manage the limited resources.

But I do need to know if I have the virus so that I can confidently support my 85-year-old mother, who has dementia and needs her daughters to turn up at weekends to give her full-time carer some time off. What am I to do? Follow the government recommendations, or do what I think is right for my family? Well, in situations like this, I always think of the CS Lewis quote: 'Integrity is doing the right thing, even when no one is watching.'

The other acid test I apply– and I would highly recommend it to anyone who is stuck with a dilemma– is to imagine your actions being published on the front page of a well-known newspaper. If you wouldn't be comfortable with that prospect, then I suspect you shouldn't do the thing you are considering. Try it out for size the next time you don't know what action to take.

THRIVE toolkit exercise: integrity

The next time you have a dilemma, jot it down in your journal and ask: 'Would I be OK with my behaviour being on the front page of a newspaper?'

In my experience, the answer quickly becomes clear. If only Dominic Cummings had considered that before he jumped in the car to go north with his family in the middle of the COVID-19 lockdown!

Celebrate along the way

Do you ever find that when things go wrong you are completely knocked sideways and find yourself in a deep hole of despair? It's as if your previous accomplishments don't exist; you convince yourself you are useless, stupid, selfish, and never going to get anywhere.

I had one client I worked with recently who felt she should have been demoted after a setback!

I hope, if this happens to you, that you will make sure you have completed the exercises in the SELF section that will help build your strong foundation.

But another thing to do to stop these setbacks becoming all-consuming is to make sure that you celebrate along the way.

When you celebrate along the way, you're putting down markers that you can go back to and reassure yourself that you did a good job and you accomplished something. If you don't celebrate, the chances are that you will move swiftly onto the next challenge without looking back – onwards and upwards, pushing yourself forward without pausing for thought or reflection.

But when you do stop and celebrate, you give yourself that moment to really appreciate what you and your colleagues have done. Acknowledging the hard work, the long hours, the creativity you accessed, the problems you solved and the people you helped.

Often, what you managed to do was no mean feat, yet so often people don't stop and appreciate it. What did you learn from that experience – about yourself, others, the way to do things, the way not to do things? When you don't stop to celebrate, you can miss these valuable lessons.

And having these markers firmly placed in your past can keep those foundations in place when things go wrong and you start to doubt yourself. Even when things don't go well, it doesn't take away the fact that you did X, Y and Z.

However, it's not always easy to remember X, Y and Z in your time of need.

That's why I recommend an accomplishments folder or pot: somewhere you can put a note you have written or an email you received about something you have accomplished. By having a place to gather all these accomplishments as they happen, you know where to go if you need a pick-me-up, or reassurance that you're not actually rubbish or some form of low-life.

I have a large glass jug in the kitchen. I encourage all my family to jot down their accomplishments and put them in the jug. Every so often we empty it and read about all the things that have gone well over the last year, and celebrate them all over again. Often, we have almost forgotten about some of the amazing things we've done, and it's a delight and a real tonic to remember them.

THRIVE toolkit exercise:

celebrate

- Decide where you will keep track of your accomplishments. Should it be a physical place, like a hanging folder or pot, or an electronic location?

- Spend some time reflecting over the last year or two and gather some accomplishments that you don't want to forget.

- What were you proud of?

- How did you really show off your talents?

- WWW – what worked well? And what do you want to do more of?

- What difference did this accomplishment make?

- Now keep going. As you accomplish things going forward, big or small, take a moment to make a note of them and pop them in your special place.

- In times of trouble or doubt, look at your accomplishments and remind yourself of how it felt.

The power of 'acting as if'

Were you brought up with the phrase 'Seeing is believing'? I certainly was. My father was a very logical thinker, so that transferred over to his map of the world. But I don't believe in those ideas any more; in fact, I believe quite the opposite.

When I have believed something at my core – even though I couldn't see it – if my faith didn't waiver, it was only a matter of time before it came into my life. I have done that with my homes, partners, boats, jobs and promotions.

But a light bulb has just gone off: it wasn't until I started writing this chapter that I realised I haven't yet believed I could be a respected author. No wonder writing this book has been so challenging! As soon as I recognised that today, I did a guided meditation and I now feel quite differently about writing.

The other phrase you've already heard from me is 'be careful what you wish for', but it's no good giving lip service to that idea and hoping things will get better, while all along worrying that they won't. The magic of 'acting as if' doesn't work that way. There is a difference between knowing something and living it.

When you live your life trusting that positive things will happen to you, even if you can't see how right now, your life will change. Maybe you'd like to have a strong belief that you're going to be OK financially, that you will be successful, that a senior management position is in your DNA.

But if you actually have the belief that 'I'll believe it when I see it', it will hold you back, limit your potential and negate the power of your mind, imagination and intention to allow and create what you want in life.

How are you behaving right now? Are you acting as if the things you want in life will happen? What if you were to act as if you already have everything you need to be successful, happy and fulfilled – which you do, by the way!

Over the years I have spent a lot of time waiting in the lobbies of large prestigious firms. I can be there quite some time, and however tempting it has been to sit there buried in my phone, I have chosen to play another game: I just watch. I watch the employees coming and going and I see whether I can detect the character of the place. What's the morale of the employees? Who is in the executive suite and who is not? I have to say, this has kept me very enjoyably entertained over the years.

Anyway, why am I sharing this? What has it got to do with 'acting as if'?

Client story:
Namesh, acting as if

A few years ago I was working with a client called Namesh, getting him ready for promotion to director level. He believed he should have been made up as a director ages ago, as his financial results were second to none.

However, he didn't look or act the part, so I could understand at some level why he hadn't made it. Don't get me wrong; I am not saying I agree with it, just that it didn't surprise me.

While I was working with Namesh, I asked him whether he believed he should be a director. After a small hesitation, he said, 'Absolutely – I beat everyone when it comes to getting money into the firm.' But that wasn't the question I asked, so I asked him again: 'Do you really believe you should be a director?'

He admitted that he wasn't sure. I asked him then whether he thought he acted like a director. To that he answered, 'No, but I will when I am made up!' I then went on to share with him that he was missing a trick. If he started 'acting as if' he was a director now, he would behave differently, think differently and get a different response from others.

At this point, Namesh wasn't convinced, so I invited him down to the shiny marble lobby of his well-known firm to play the game with me. We sat in the lobby, on smart black leather sofas, to watch his colleagues come and go. I suggested that I would be able to guess the directors without him telling me. He was astonished that I guessed nine out of every ten directors who went by.

Next, I got him to really look and notice what was different about his director-level colleagues. How did they hold themselves? How did they walk? What did they look like? Soon, he was able to see several ways in which they were different from the way *he* currently came across.

With this new information in mind, he decided to change some of his behaviours and 'act as if' he was already a director. He was amazed at how different it felt – what he believed about himself, how assertive he was in meetings and how confident he felt. To cut a long story short, he made it to director, and he puts this down in part to 'acting as if'.

Whatever you want– whether it's a promotion, a soul mate or a new home in a better neighbourhood– my advice is to 'act as if' you already have the thing you want. With that approach, your beliefs and identity change and your behaviour follows. You will be amazed how quickly your life can turn around.

Your best self

As you look back over your career and life, I have no doubt you will be able to remember moments when you were your 'best self' – times when you were on fire and seemed to be able to achieve effortlessly.

We have all had these moments, however fleeting, but I suspect most of them have happened by chance rather than by design. Time, opportunities and people have conspired to come together at a perfect moment for you to be at your best.

What would it be like, though, if you could engineer these moments and create them more often? What would life be like then? What would you be able to achieve if you regularly functioned at your best?

I know it's possible, and it's more likely to happen if you practise the wisdom in this book; if you know who you are and have done the exercises in the SELF section; if you have mastered your relationship with TIME and are able to achieve more and worry less; if you have also mastered your relationship with OTHERS and are able to have the impact and influence you want. If you also have your high PERFORMANCE in mind, you will automatically increase your chances of being your best self and help it to happen more often.

But what if you asked yourself this question every day:

'How can I be my best self today?'

By asking that question, you automatically get yourself into a more effective state and step up differently to the challenges ahead.

Perhaps you have a tough meeting and, to be your 'best self', you need to be thoroughly prepared and ready for action, having thought through all the possible angles and different challenges you might be presented with. Stepping into your assertive, confident state before you walk in will serve you.

Or maybe you've got an appraisal to do and you know the other person is feeling vulnerable. It's going to take patience and understanding to do this appraisal well, and it wouldn't be wise to turn up late and feel rushed. Doing some box breathing and connecting with the present moment will help you to be your 'best self'.

Maybe it's a family member's special day, and to be your 'best self' you need to finish work early and leave your work at the office (physically and mentally) to be the best parent/sibling/son or daughter.

By consciously thinking about how you can be your best self today, you are already getting in the groove.

**THRIVE toolkit exercise:
be your best self**

- Grab your journal and write down a goal you want to achieve in the future. Make it as clear and vivid as you can. It might be something like 'I want to be promoted to director in three years' time', or 'I want to have found my life partner and have started a family', or 'I want to be fit and flexible, weighing X kilograms, in a year's time'. Write down your goal in as much detail as possible.

- Next, amplify your desire for this goal by noting down how life will be different for you and those around you when this goal is accomplished:

  – Perhaps the promotion will mean you feel more financially secure and that will have positive implications for your nearest and dearest.

  – Maybe having the family you desire will make you and your partner uber happy. You will be very much in love and aligned with your life goals and parenting ideas.

  – Possibly when you are the weight you want to be, and fit and flexible too, you will have much more energy to do whatever you want.

- Now consider what strengths you will need to demonstrate to get there. What aspects of your best self will you need to tap into? For example, 'I will need to be focused and determined and not take my eye off the prize of promotion. It will take courage and hard work.' Or 'I will need to look after myself and balance my work, so I have time to have a social life. It will take discipline and at the same time a sense of fun.'

- Notice how different it feels now as you consider your goal.

I would love to hear what goals you have set yourself and the impact these goals are having on your life. Please do share them with me on **sarah@sarahsparks.co.uk**.

Leaving a legacy

When people think about leaving a legacy, they often think about finances. But that's not the legacy I am talking about here. I mean a legacy that will last much longer than any financial gift. I am talking about the imprint you make on others.

Whether you like it or not, you are a role model to others all the time. If you're a parent, your kids are watching your every move and will learn to walk and talk just like you do. More than that; they learn and emulate (or reject) your values and beliefs, too. All of this is happening outside of their conscious awareness, but don't kid yourself; it's happening, for sure.

And you don't have to be a parent for this to happen.

We are all looking out for role models to either emulate or shun all the time. The people you admire and the people you despise are all sending you messages and nudges about how to live your life. We pick up their beliefs and behaviours which dictate what's acceptable around here—good and bad.

The question is: who do you want to be a role model for? Who are you already being a role model for? Your children? Your younger colleagues who are coming up the ranks behind you? Your community? Your peers?

What sort of legacy are you already leaving? Is it one you'll be proud of at the end of your days? Thinking about those people you want to be a role model for, would you be happy if their opinion of you was written on your gravestone? What would it say? Would the words of your epitaph represent your best self or not?

Now, I am not saying you need to be perfect—not at all. I am saying you need to be human and be conscious of the legacy you might be leaving.

When I was working with Simon, a senior leader in a well-known investment bank, this concept of legacy hadn't crossed his mind. He was known for being a really hard taskmaster and he took no prisoners when it came to his team.

The people who worked for him felt that he ruled by fear and were often so frightened that they were like rabbits in headlights, not knowing what to do for the best, so staying frozen and doing nothing. That used to infuriate Simon and often resulted in him having a hissy fit that would create even more fear in those around him. Clearly his behaviour was not bringing out the best in his team and needed to change.

When I brought up the subject of his legacy and what people might remember him for, he went silent. He was a decent guy with high ideals, and clearly successful, but he would need to change his ways if he wanted to continue this success going forward.

I asked him what he wanted to be remembered for, and he came up with the following ideas: a radical leader who changed how things were done; someone who others wanted to work with, to be part of changing things; someone who worked hard and made it to the top.

He was quick to notice that he needed to behave differently and get his team on board if he was going to be successful.

Now you've probably heard the phrase 'a leopard doesn't change his spots', and to some degree this was true: Simon didn't change overnight. But he did now have this idea of legacy in his mind and took conscious steps to change the way he led others. As I said to him, 'You can't be a leader unless you have a following.'

When it comes to considering your legacy, here are some ideas that I think make the difference.

- Practise what you preach.

- Apologise when you make a mistake. You don't need to be perfect – be human.

- Say what you mean and mean what you say – follow through.

- Treat others with respect, at home and at work.

- Be consistent.

"Legacy is not leaving something for people but leaving something in people."

PETER STROPLE

THRIVE toolkit exercise:
leaving a legacy

- Grab your journal and write down what you want your legacy to be. What do you want to be remembered for?

- If you died tomorrow, is that the thing others would say?

- If not, what do you need to do to leave the legacy you want?

- List three habits or behaviours you'd like to change. Make them small and actionable. For example, 'get to bed 30 minutes earlier so I am less snappy with others', 'seek first to understand before I chip in with my point of view', 'do a small good deed every day'.

- How will you remind yourself regularly to do these things? What visual nudge could you create that will remind you?

Summary of PERFORMANCE

This chapter was all about thinking ahead and setting yourself up for sustainable high performance and being your best self. You can master the rest (SELF, TIME and OTHERS), but unless you have your long term in mind you can easily get knocked off course and find yourself stuck in a rut with life passing you by.

Spend a moment reflecting on just how much you have learnt about yourself and others so far in this book. Who else in your world needs to know this information? How about you share this book after you have finished? Or, if you can't bear to part with it and want to keep it for reference, how about buying them a copy?

Here's the QR code you need to make it easy.

They will be forever grateful, and so will I!

In this chapter you have learnt:

Step 1: Making better choices

The importance of:

▶ Keeping your long-term performance in mind

▶ Creating certainty

▶ Seeing setbacks as opportunities

▶ Your mental form

▶ Using biofeedback technology.

Step 2: Setting yourself up for long-term success

The importance of:

▶ Planning ahead

▶ The company you keep

▶ Having an accountability partner

▶ Choosing happiness

▶ Integrity

▶ Celebrating

▶ 'Acting as if'

▶ Your best self

▶ Leaving a legacy.

And added the following tools to your THRIVE toolkit:

SURVIVE TOOLKIT	THRIVE TOOLKIT
STEP ONE: MAKING BETTER CHOICES	
Mental form	Focus on the solution
	Mental form
STEP TWO: SETTING YOURSELF UP FOR LONG-TERM SUCCESS	
Planning ahead	Accountability
The people around you	Integrity
	Celebrate
	Be your best self
	Leaving a legacy

IN SUMMARY

Congratulations! You have made it to the end. You've stuck with it and have taken steps towards thriving and having a sustainable way of working and living. If you have managed to complete the exercises, I applaud you; hopefully, you have a journal full of notes and reflections. And if you haven't, I applaud you too and hope that you have found some nuggets in this book that have resonated and have been useful.

Let's see how far you have come; I am hoping you will be pleasantly surprised. Grab your journal and notes, and without looking back at earlier entries, complete another wheel of life exercise (see page 121).

Score the following areas out of 10 – how satisfied are you with each one right now?

- Career

- Money

- Health

- Family and friends

- Significant other

- Personal growth

- Fun and recreation

- Physical environment

Now take a look at the scores you wrote down before. What's different now? How do you feel overall? If you've done the exercises in this book, the chances are that many of your scores will have improved. Celebrate– but don't rest on your laurels. What's next? What would you like the scores to be in six months or a year from now? You know the drill. By doing this exercise regularly you will not only become more aware, but you will also have a direction of travel and know that you are on your way.

The reality is that we cannot change the world, so the likelihood is that you will not be able to stop the stress and pressures of your life. But you can change the way you respond to them. I do hope now that by understanding the stress response, you will respond differently and will now focus more on your recovery and bringing down those stress hormones as often as you can by using the STOP process. There are lots of ways of doing that, and this book is full of them; choose the ones that work for you.

By taking action every day and implementing some of the suggestions in this book to help you rest and recover, you will be in the minority and on the road to thriving by establishing a sustainable way of working, away from the risk of burnout.

By keeping your long-term thriving in mind every day, you will make better choices and reap the rewards.

Keep going, and Choose to Thrive. Remember to STOP!

"Nothing will work unless you do."

MAYA ANGELOU

Connect with Sarah:

www.linkedin.com/in/choose2thrive

www.sarahsparks.co.uk

To help you work through the exercises in this book get your free resource pack at **www.sarahsparks.co.uk/ideas/download-your-workbook-here/**

If you have enjoyed this book, there's a variety of ways you can work with Sarah to embed the learning and accelerate your THRIVING:

One-to-one coaching

For those who are ready to push themselves outside their comfort zone and step up to the next level, one-to-one coaching could be for you. Please note that Sarah only takes on a few coaching clients each year.

"Before I met Sarah life was fast paced, successful, full of juggling life and work demands yet inwardly (and probably outwardly) exhausted, surviving on instinct and quick decisions, and with hindsight not so much fun. With Sarah's help I have now been able to set my compass to have a much greater balance in work and life, and have the mind space to keep developing and thriving. Thank you."

PAUL COATES – HEAD OF DEBT ADVISORY AND STRUCTURED FINANCE, GLOBAL COMMERCIAL REAL ESTATE COMPANY

"I previously found it extremely difficult to switch off. Working with Sarah has helped me develop a personal toolkit to thrive at work. I appreciate downtime and home life, and I am much more effective at hybrid working."

PHILIP ANDERSON – COO FINANCIAL SERVICES COMPANY

"Working with Sarah changed my life. She helped me see that running on stress was running away from myself and my essence and that was only half showing up in the world. She gave me the keys to live with more authenticity and permission to show up for life as myself. I'm not overestimating it when I say she saved my life- thank you Sarah, for what you bring to the world."

JULIETTE MORGAN – SENIOR EXECUTIVE
AT LEADING UK PROPERTY COMPANY

Invite Sarah to speak

As an award-winning speaker and experienced panellist, Sarah will create a thought-provoking and practical experience for your audience, so that they come away inspired and ready to implement what they have learnt to improve their current situation.

"Thanks so much for your incredible intervention at the conference; a spellbinding presentation, and feedback has been excellent so mission very much accomplished!"

DAVID WHELDON – CMO & EXECUTIVE COMMITTEE MEMBER, RBS

"Very much enjoyed your talk at the conference – a stand-out session in a very high-quality day!"

"You made the day! I thoroughly enjoyed the style and content of your session. I'm not sure if you had access to the conference app but the newsfeed was going wild! Lots of personal commitments relating to your SMART ideas."

"Your session landed really well yesterday. Thanks for sharing."

"I was watching your slot at the C&M conference – I was absolutely gripped and in awe."

ACKNOWLEDGEMENTS

Thank you to all of you who have contributed to this book.

The senior executives I have interviewed and who have been willing to share their experiences so openly.

My colleagues and clients, past, present and future who have enabled me to learn and grow and continue to do so

Theo and Ellen who have lived through this journey and have always been beside me.

Simon for his continued friendship, support and encouragement.

Carole, for doing a fantastic job of ensuring I get my voice out in the world and always going the extra mile.

Ali and Leila from Known Publishing, who have guided me through this process and helped me to finally get this book into print.

ENDNOTES

1 2020 Gallup Global Emotions Report

2 NIMH Chronic Illness and Mental Health, reviewed 10/15/2020

3 AON & IPSOS 2021 Global Wellbeing Survey

4 Qualtrics COVID and Mental Health Survey 2020

5 Research carried out in November 2020 by Springhealth

6 World Economic Forum. *It's time to end the stigma around mental health in the workplace.*

7 World Economic Forum (2011)

8 Accenture/This is Me Report, December 2019

9 http://scitechconnect.elsevier.com/stress-health-epidemic-21st-century/

10 https://www.bitc.org.uk/report/mental-health-at-work-2019-time-to-take-ownership/

11 https://assets.publishing.service.gov.uk/government/uploads/system/uploads/attachment_data/file/658145/thriving-at-work-stevenson-farmer-review.pdf

12 https://www.thelancet.com/commissions/global-mental-health

13 Donnellan, A. Masters of universe, victims of high stress. *Sunday Times*, 19 June 2016.

14 https://www.hse.gov.uk/statistics/causdis/

15 https://www.hse.gov.uk/statistics/causdis/stress.pdf

16 https://www.sleepfoundation.org/how-sleep-works/how-much-sleep-do-we-really-need

17 Hafner M, Stepanek M, Taylor J et al. Why sleep matters – the economic costs of insufficient sleep. *Rand Health Q.* 6(4): 11 (2017).

18 Van Dongen HPA, Rogers N, Dinges DF. Sleep debt: theoretical and empirical issues. *Sleep and Biological Rhythms* 1: 5–13 (2003).

19 https://www.health.harvard.edu/blog/regular-exercise-changes-brain-improve-memory-thinking-skills-201404097110

20 https://www.alzheimers.org.uk/about-dementia/risk-factors-and-prevention/physical-exercise

21 https://www.timetothink.com/thinking-environment/the-ten-components/

22 https://www.forbes.com/sites/travisbradberry/2013/03/11/the-art-of-saying-no/

23 https://www.washingtonpost.com/news/inspired-life/wp/2015/06/01/interruptions-at-work-can-cost-you-up-to-6-hours-a-day-heres-how-to-avoid-them/

24 Mehrabian, A. Communication without words. *Psychology Today*, 2 (9): 52–55 (1968).

25 Cialdini, RB. *Influence: The Psychology of Persuasion.* Melbourne: Business Library, 1984.

Printed in Great Britain
by Amazon

68850929R00194